PRAISE FOR *TINY BUDDHA*

"How can we find happiness and peace—right now, right here? In her engaging, thought-provoking book *Tiny Buddha*, Lori Deschene explores this enormous question to help readers grapple with challenges like money, love, pain, control, and meaning, in order to find greater happiness."

—Gretchen Rubin, author of *The Happiness Project*

"Lori is one of a kind. Her amazing heart and wisdom shine through in everything she writes! I am a HUGE fan of *Tiny Buddha*, and I'm constantly inspired by Lori and her work."

—Mastin Kipp, founder of The Daily Love
(thedailylove.com)

"There's nothing tiny about the extra-large dose of awesome stuffed into Lori's writing. Read it and feel good about the world."

—Neil Pasricha, founder and author of 1000
Awesome Things and *The Book of Awesome*

"Few people in our time have more passionately or more creatively applied wisdom teachings to a new digital generation than Lori Deschene. I am continually inspired by her writing, and also by her sincere dedication to learnii

tremendously fortunate to have had the chance to get to know her work through *Tiny Buddha,* and to know her as a person. Both embody the same essential truths."

—Soren Gordhamer, founder and author of *Wisdom 2.0*

"Lori Deschene doesn't claim to be anybody's guru. But it's that lack of pretense and her total candor—how she tells her own often-wild story without flinching—that is so magnetic, inviting a sense of ease with our own wrinkles, too, and fostering a sense of personal possibility. As she asks: Are you ready to be free?"

—Margaret Roach, author of *And I Shall Have Some Peace There*

"I spent months retweeting posts from a mystery handle called @tinybuddha. I wasn't the only one: Hundreds of thousands of people followed the daily messages. I was intrigued and made it a point to meet the woman behind the message. Today, Lori Deschene is a friend and fellow author who spreads truth and inspiration throughout the Twittersphere, her blog, and now her new book! Lori has shifted the energy of the Internet with her loving daily posts and now she is sharing more with the world through her incredible book!"

—Gabrielle Bernstein, author of *The Universe Has Your Back*

"*Tiny Buddha* is a moving and insightful synthesis of evocative stories and ancient wisdom applied to modern life. A great read!"

—Jonathan Fields, author of *Uncertainty*

TINY
BUDDHA

SIMPLE WISDOM
for LIFE'S HARD QUESTIONS

LORI DESCHENE

Founder of Tiny Buddha

Conari Press

This edition first published in 2017 by Conari Press, an imprint of
Red Wheel/Weiser, LLC
65 Parker Street, Suite 7
Newburyport, MA 01950
www.redwheelweiser.com

ISBN: 978-1-57324-709-2
Library of Congress Cataloging-in-Publication Data
Deschene, Lori.
  Tiny Buddha, simple wisdom for life's hard questions / Lori Deschene.
     p. cm.
  Includes bibliographical references and index.
  ISBN 978-1-57324-506-7 (hardback)
  1. Mind and body. I. Title.
  BF161.D453 2012
  158—dc23

2011036925

Cover design by Jim Warner
Interior by Steve Amarillo / Urban Design LLC
Typeset in Sabon and Futura
Calligraphy: Chinese meaning - wisdom © Chubbster / Shutterstock; Buddha: God of
Happiness © tomgigabite / Bigstock

Printed in Canada
MAR
10 9 8 7 6 5 4 3 2 1

DEDICATION

~~~~~~~~~~~~~~~~~~~

In loving memory of Henry "Grandpa Joe" Santoro.
This one's for you, too!

CONTENTS

INTRODUCTION

~~~~~~~~~~~~~~~

In March of 2007, when Twitter exploded at the South by Southwest Festival, more than 60,000 tweets addressed the question, "What are you doing?" At the time, I was certain I'd sooner post my organs for auction on eBay than choose a Twitter handle. I didn't see any benefit in using technology to narrate my life as it happened. Why would I want to update my social circle—let alone strangers—on my most mundane daily activities? I assumed that if I joined, I'd bore my friends with TMI and have less to discuss when I saw them in person—they'd already know I ate a Rice Krispies Treat at ten, practiced yoga at lunch, and seriously considered cutting my bangs at four. I thought I couldn't live mindfully if I traced my steps with a digital bread-crumb trail. If I *did* use the web to share random details about my everyday life, I'd want to answer a far more interesting question than, "What are you doing?"

In 2008, I realized how badly I'd underestimated that question. What was I doing? I was writing for a series of websites that didn't mean anything to me on a personal level. I was trying to figure out how to be an independent, valuable part of society after years of crawling, one inch at a time, out of self-loathing and depression—an ascent that felt as knuckle-draggingly prolonged as humans' evolution from apes. I was for all intents and purposes doing a lot better, but I was not feeling better about the things I was doing. And I was drowning in spiritual texts and self-help books looking for answers everywhere outside myself. What I wasn't doing was living an empowered life, driven by my passions and guided by my gut instincts.

After years of obsessing over who I was, it felt empowering to shift my focus to what I was doing. Suddenly I was considering that maybe Twitter wasn't as superficial as I thought it had to be. It could be like tofu and take the flavor of whatever it's marinated in—and I could mix it up as my taste buds demanded. That's the beauty of Twitter: each tweeter decides which questions to answer, and they can be as helpful and meaningful as you make them. Asking the questions that shape our lives and exploring potential solutions—now that was something worth doing.

The simultaneous lack and abundance of answers is the answer. "

I had lots of questions to answer: What makes a person happy? How can you live a meaningful life? How do you move forward after a poor decision or disappointment that eats away at your sense of possibility? How can you push yourself out of your comfort zone and live the life you dream about? How can you find a sense of security in a world with so many unknowns? The list was endless, really.

No matter what religion we follow, what politics we support, what family we were born into, or where we've placed our roots, we all deal with universal problems. Regardless of our differences, we all live our lives around the same questions. How we answer them dictates the choices we'll make and what kind of person we'll be from moment to moment. Some answers are clichés that look great on paper but don't actually breathe when we inflate them and try to find a pulse. Others seem implausible and yet make a world of sense when we step inside them and wrap them around our circumstances. And others still can feel absolute for what seems like an eternity until life cross-examines them and reminds us how fragile most answers are.

Was I merely regurgitating words that felt good or feeling good about doing something with them? **//**

The reality is there are very few concrete, one-size-fits-all answers to the big questions. According to Socrates, accepting that is the foundation to true wisdom. There's so much we can't know, understand, or predict in life. Yet if we learn to listen to ourselves and then to stop listening long enough to simply be in the world, open and available, the answers can seem so clear—*answer*, really. The real answer is that there are an infinite number of possibilities that we can explore to be happy, connected, engaged, and free. The simultaneous lack and abundance of answers *is* the answer.

Tiny Buddha evolved from that idea—the prospect of exploring different possibilities and then doing something with them so we can learn for ourselves what's right for each of us.

They say we teach what we need to learn, and this has been true for me. When I started tweeting a daily quote through @tinybuddha, I addressed the questions that felt most paralyzing in my world. I looked for quotes about letting go of stress and anxiety because I'd carried so much around for years it oozed from my skin, like a little too much garlic. I read countless books, highlighter in hand, looking for insights about being happy in the present because I'd spent so much time obsessing over the past and worrying over the future that I disbelieved it was possible to liberate the now. Once upon a time, I thought mindfulness was a comforting illusion—something spoon-fed to me like Santa, the American Dream, and free lunches.

After a year of sharing these simple ideas in a one-day-at-a-time format, with the @tinybuddha follower count growing into the thousands (now more than two hundred thousand), I reassessed: What *was* I doing? Was I merely regurgitating words that felt good or feeling good about doing something with them?

I considered that maybe lots of other people just like me were sitting at their computers wondering if they felt proud of how they answered the question, "What are you doing?" Reading an inspiring quote doesn't guarantee inspired action, particularly in an information-overloaded world where many of us spend our days inertly glued to technology. Sometimes when we gorge ourselves on meaningful words, we fall into an intention coma—too overwhelmed by other people's thoughts to identify the right choices for ourselves.

So I developed *TinyBuddha.com* in September 2009, where anyone can contribute tips and stories about wisdom in everyday life. Since then, I've watched a community grow from one to more than I ever could have imagined (more than three million unique visits to the website and more than fifty thousand Facebook and two hundred thousand Twitter followers), all of us looking to learn and share wisdom— people of all ages and backgrounds from all over the globe united by the same sense of uncertainty and a determination to thrive regardless.

That's what brought me to this book: a fascination with the questions that connect us and the wisdom—conventional or otherwise—that guides the decisions we make each day.

What You'll Get from this Book

Nearly one thousand people responded when I began asking life's hardest questions on Twitter, planning to create a collaborative book. As I read through their responses, I realized the answers fell into distinct categories of ideas. While there were occasionally responses that didn't parallel anyone else's, for the most part, the tweets grouped themselves into sections.

I didn't influence the responses to fit an agenda; I shaped my exploration around the suggestions in the tweets. Just like friends of Tiny Buddha in all its forms have guided *TinyBuddha.com*, their insights form the backbone of this book. Since many of the tweets were quite similar, I chose a handful that aligned with each shared perspective. From there, I dug through the archives of my memories to weigh the ideas against my own experiences and then dived into books and articles that shed further light on these ideas.

Throughout each section, you'll find a number of tips and exercises to help you take action on what you've read. Now, I never do exercises as I read a book—not even when an author writes, "I know you probably don't usually do exercises in books, but please do these!" So I have a different suggestion for you: Highlight the ones that seem useful to you, and when you find yourself in a relevant situation in life, come back to them and take action then.

I'm not a huge fan of vague, flowery, New Age jargon, so I've gone to great effort to keep this book practical and rooted in reality. I recently read a blog post about succeeding in sales. The author suggested that the best way to sell anything is to position it as the magic bullet—the ultimate answer or method to doing something that we all want to do in life but don't want to work for, like losing weight, getting a fulfilling job, or finding happiness. He offered some supporting information to show that we more often spend money on worthless things that seem like quick fixes than on proven systems that require time and effort. Despite the advice, which I suspect holds some truth, I will tell you this book is *not* a magic bullet.

Sometimes when we gorge ourselves on meaningful words, we fall into an intention coma—too overwhelmed by other people's thoughts to identify the right choices for ourselves. "

This is not a guide of absolute answers. It's crowd sourced wisdom, often supported by scientific, psychological, and sociological research, that may help you experience meaning, happiness, and peace *right now*, regardless of your circumstances. It's a reflection of and on popular opinion and an examination of the ways we can leverage what we know *and* what we don't for our individual and collective well-being.

Sharing parts of my personal journey was a lot like doing intermittent cartwheels naked on my front lawn—my stories might be brief, but I certainly put it all out there. In the spirit of that same authenticity, I want to be clear that I am not an expert on living wisely. I suspect that if I presented myself that way, I'd immediately convey my ignorance, because wisdom is a lifelong pursuit. I didn't write this book sitting at a cherrywood desk in my psychiatry office or in between personal development seminars I host around the globe. I wrote this from the shabby couch I bought on Craigslist while running a Twitter account and a website that appear to help a lot of people. I acknowledge my nonexpert status not to undermine my ideas but to remind you up front that we all possess the same capacity to reason, learn, and then act based on what makes sense to us.

You'll notice I didn't ask questions directly relating to religion. I suspected a lot of the questions would inspire spiritual discussions and decided to broach the subjects that way. You may also notice that none of the tweets have any typical Twitter slang—no abbreviations or emoticons. For the sake of reading ease, I corrected misspellings and omitted excessive punctuation. Lastly, you may wonder why I didn't start each section with a *TinyBuddha.com* quote, as I do on the site. The simple reason is that I wanted this book to explore our collective understandings, which often parallel many of those same ideas.

I want you to read this knowing that you are not alone. Whatever question you're asking yourself right now, someone else somewhere else—but probably a lot closer than you think—is wondering the very same thing. If you search Twitter for emotional words like happy or frustrated—as I tend to do when coming up with blog topics—you'll find a seemingly infinite number of similar thoughts, feelings, problems, observations, and conclusions.

The questions are what unite us. It's up to me, and it's up to you, to identify and use the answers that empower each of us as individuals.

PAIN

WHY IS THERE SUFFERING IN THE WORLD?

~~~~~~~~~~~~~~~~~~~~~~~~~~~~~~~~~~~~

No matter who you are, no matter what you have, no matter what you've achieved, you've hurt at some point in your life. Of the six universal emotions psychologists have identified—happiness, sadness, surprise, fear, disgust, and anger—the majority indicate pain.

Most of us know that what our grandmothers said was true: "This too shall pass." But it doesn't always seem that way in the moment. When all those pain-induced hormones flood your body, pushing you into survivor mode, it can feel like some catastrophic turn of events has irreparably damaged your life—like your world has permanently fallen apart. If you don't worry hard enough, things might never change. If you don't get angry enough, you'll be accepting that what happened was okay. If you don't get bitter enough, you're opening yourself up to more of that same disastrous hurt.

Right?

No. It doesn't work that way. No matter how justified we feel in our emotions, stewing in them is never the answer to making them go away. Stressing by itself can't create a solution—*any* solution, let alone a rational one. Anger doesn't punish the people or circumstances that hurt us; it punishes us. And bitterness doesn't protect us from pain down the line; if anything, it invites it.

Emotions are not resolutions—and yet we have to let ourselves feel them. Suppressing emotional pain more often than not just creates more of it. This is where it gets confusing: If we're not supposed to resist our feelings, how do we know when to let them go? How can we both allow ourselves to feel what we need to feel and be sure we don't let the present moment pass us by?

In 2003, I sublet a small, unfurnished studio in New York City for a few weeks to figure out how I'd survive if I moved there to pursue my acting dreams. It was in August, and the Times Square area was like a sauna crammed with people sitting arm-to-arm, on laps, and on laps on top of laps, except no one was actually sitting still—we were all trying to get to different places with that New York sense of urgency.

A couple hours after I got the apartment keys, I headed out to hit up the ATM and pick up groceries and other supplies. While I was on my way to the corner store, Manhattan went dark. I didn't know it at the time, but New York was part of a multistate power outage. The traffic lights went black, which gave pedestrians the green light to storm the streets, causing massive traffic jams. People began rushing into convenience stores to get provisions for the hours ahead. It was total chaos, and I felt panicked.

I didn't have any cash—or food or candles or a plan of attack. So I sat on a curb, leaned up against a mailbox, and tried to control my breath. Apparently I was more gasping and panting than inhaling and exhaling because a man squatted down, put his hand on my shoulder, and said, "Honey, are you okay?" I didn't see that coming—and I also didn't expect he'd listen to me ramble about just arriving, not having any cash, and fearing I might need to sell my body for a sandwich, a flashlight, or both. Without flinching, he gave me $5 and pointed me toward a store. Crammed with panicked, sweating people, the inside reeked, like body odor and cottage cheese after extended time in a beach bag. I was able to grab a bottle of water, but I didn't have enough for food, and the options were getting slim as other people rushed to grab what they could. The woman behind the register gave me a roasted half-duck and took down my credit card info to charge at a later date. I had food and water; now all I needed was light. Naturally, $5 flashlights were going for over $20 a pop on the street—good old supply and demand. So I ducked into a restaurant, told the bartender my story, and left with seven tea lights.

It was increasingly crowded on the route to my apartment, so I paused in Times Square, which was kind of awesome in its darkness—now that I knew all my basic needs were met. It was like going backstage before a Broadway play, seeing the man-made framework behind the illusion of magic. In fact, it was very similar, since all kinds of people were gathering around musicians putting on impromptu shows. I struck up a conversation with the girl next to me, telling her how surprised I was that New Yorkers were so friendly and willing to lend a hand, even with their own needs to attend to. She said New Yorkers band together during crises, particularly after 9/11. They look out for each other, and they're a lot more compassionate and helpful than the cliché might indicate.

I can't remember her name, but I'll never forget what she told me next: both her father and her boyfriend died in the Twin Towers. In one day, only a couple years before our chance encounter, she lost the two people who mattered most to her in life. They say some deaths are senseless when you imagine they could have been prevented, but death rarely, if ever, makes sense—particularly not when it comes as part of something so deplorably inhumane. I looked at her sitting there, strong, intact, no different looking than I was or anyone else who hasn't known such grief. I wondered how she could go out in the daylight, looking peaceful in the world, knowing firsthand how tragedy can strike so unexpectedly. I looked deeply into her eyes in a potentially invasive way, searching for signs of pervasive inner turmoil. Having endured such a horrific tragedy, she must be a shell of a person, I thought, particularly so soon after her losses.

Then I remembered where I was right before I learned about the 9/11 attacks. I was festering in bed, six prescription bottles on my nightstand, wondering who'd come to my funeral if I died. I'd been in therapy for almost a decade, and yet I still suspected I'd spend the rest of my life feeling alone, miserable, and confined like a prisoner within the deafening cruelty of my mind. I was a chubby, overdeveloped twelve-year-old the first time a boy groped me and called me a whore in the school hallway. After years of hearing "fat slut" from both boys and girls alone and in packs and being grabbed without my consent, I'd begun to believe my consent wasn't necessary. Once, a girl from a neighboring school told me, "I've heard you're thinking of changing schools. Don't bother. Everyone everywhere knows you're a worthless whore." From that point on, I truly believed this was fact—that everyone I met somehow already knew how pathetic and worthless I was. A decade later, at twenty-two, I still felt trapped under layers of shame and regret, like dozens of lead-filled X-ray aprons piled one on top of the other. I'd tried to starve it away, stuff it away, drink it away, and fight it away, but nothing changed that I felt trapped within my offensive, unlovable skin.

I called my aunt to complain about my misery; I had a roster of regular listeners who indulged my desperation. Not a few seconds into my woe-is-me story, she asked me, "Lori, how can you be thinking about yourself? Don't you know what's happening in the world?" I didn't have any idea. I turned on the television and saw the footage. They kept showing the towers going down, like sand castles slowly crumbling, and a part of me felt like it wasn't real. I knew that people were hurting and that I should be outraged. But I'd numbed my own feelings for so long that it felt nearly impossible to feel for people far removed from me and my debilitating apathy. I'd seen therapist after psychiatrist after pharmacist; I was on antidepressants, mood stabilizers, and tranquilizers. My whole life was about making sure I didn't have to feel. But how could I see such tragedy and *not* feel? And even worse, how could I be seeing it and still be so concerned with what *I* was doing and feeling? What was wrong with me that I was so absorbed in what was wrong with me?

The truth, as messy as it sounds, is that the only way out is through. "

That's the thing about feelings: Sometimes we resist them, and then we sit around feeling more feelings about our feelings, drowning in reactive emotions. We remember what happened and wonder what, if anything, we did to provoke it. We wonder what we could have done to prevent it. We wonder if we deserved it. We think about how unfair things are and how we wish we could go back in time to change them. We think about how we handled things, and if maybe we could have made other choices to change the outcome of what it is. And then after all this resistance, we wonder what's wrong with us for struggling so much in our own self-absorption. After all, there are so many other worse things going on in the world.

The truth, as messy as it sounds, is that the only way out is through. And the only way to let go is to truly believe in the possibility of a different way of being—to know in our head and in our heart that we can live a life that doesn't revolve around having been hurt or fearing future pain. We don't always realize it when we're sitting in our own self-destructed ground zero, but there will be a day when we feel better—if we just let ourselves go through it. Everything gets better with time; how much time is up to us. It's dependent on when we choose to change the stories we tell about our lives; when we decide to spend more time creating the life we want than lamenting the hand we've been dealt; and when we realize that no one's love, forgiveness, or acceptance can be as profoundly healing as our own.

> **M**aybe if I stopped trying to control how I hurt, I'd feel a pain that would teach me what I need to do to love life more and need pain less. *"*

As I looked at my new friend, vulnerable and yet so resilient, I wanted to love and heal her. I couldn't see it, but I knew she must be cracked beneath the surface. I imagined that she cried, screamed, and wailed herself through lonesome, traumatic nights. I visualized her collapsing into the arms of people she loved—other survivors who understood. I wanted to take it all away. I wanted to save her from a suffering that I could only imagine ate away at her soul day and night. I wanted to be her Prozac. I wanted to make her numb to the reality of her losses.

Then I realized that in that moment, she didn't need a hero. In that moment, she was existing independent of her tragic past. She wasn't heaving, having flashbacks, or fighting with the injustices of the world. She was responding to what was in front of her. She was eating a salad, albeit a wilting one; listening to music she seemed to enjoy; and acknowledging me, an absolute stranger sharing a once-in-a-lifetime experience within an eerily tame Times Square. She didn't need someone to take the pain away forever, because she was taking forever one minute at a time.

We all choose from moment to moment where we focus our attention and what we tell ourselves. We're always going to want to have more of the good things, less of the bad things, and a greater sense of control over the distribution. While we can't control that life involves hurting, we can control how long we endure it and what we do with it.

To a large degree, it's irrelevant to question why we have to suffer, since that just prolongs acceptance of what is. But it's human nature to want to understand. If we're going to form conclusions, they might as well be empowering ones that help us work through pain and let go. With that in mind, I asked on Twitter, "Why is there suffering in the world?"

Pain is a teacher

Suffering should be used as a teacher. This teacher will teach you about yourself and the world around you. ~@d1sco_very

There is suffering in the world to make people wiser and stronger. ~@ittybittyfaerie

Without suffering no lessons will be learned; without suffering none will be necessary. ~@andrew2pack

We experience suffering to understand and realize our true strength. Pain leads us to improve our quality of life and open to love. ~@ditzl

Do not seek justification for suffering. There is none. Accept its existence and learn from it. ~@Mark10023

It's a natural human instinct to resist pain and to avoid its causes at all costs. In fact, we experience a biological response to perceived danger that tells us when to run for our lives—or in some cases, when to sit around stressing about our inability to run as quickly as we'd like. Just like an animal senses it might be eaten and receives an increase in adrenaline, enabling escape, early humans also developed a fine-tuned fight-or-flight response to survive in a dangerous world. It originates in the amygdala—the part of the brain that creates fear conditioning.

The only difference between us now and us then is that instead of being attacked by lions, as we may have been centuries ago, we're more likely to get in romantic squabbles or professional confrontations. More often than not, when we start kicking and screaming, there's little if any real threat; there's the just the fear of something potentially uncomfortable. We know intellectually that a disagreement or challenge at work won't kill us—and that stressing won't do anything to change what was or what will be. But we've conditioned ourselves to fight for control over our circumstances; and when that control seems to slip away, we panic. It's an ironic way of avoiding discomfort, but sometimes we make ourselves miserable to be sure that nothing or no one else can. We choose to hurt ourselves through stress and dread just to be sure we're prepared when something else could potentially hurt us.

> **W**e can take almost anything that hurts and recycle it into something good once we're ready to learn from it. **//**

On the other end of the spectrum, we've historically romanticized pain. We're always consuming survivor stories, watching movies and online videos about success after extreme adversity, and channeling our inner Nietzsche—telling ourselves that what doesn't kill us only makes us stronger. To some degree, this is good, because we're reminding ourselves that it *is* possible to bounce back after a difficult time. But it's almost as if we imagine the greater the pain, the greater the spirit; or the harder the journey, the more rewarding the destination. It's as if we believe the one who hurts the most learns the most and has the most to give the world. Or perhaps we linger in the exhausting act of trying to control the chaos because that allows us to avoid acknowledging the gap between who we are and who we want to be.

In *The Power of Now*, Eckhart Tolle explains that we hold on to problems because they give us a sense of identity. This has been true for me. For years, I focused all my pain into the will to wither away. After weeks of surviving on a small selection of Sweet'N Low–flavored, low-calorie blandness, I'd feel shooting pains in my chest, like my heart was trying to escape its prison. My abdominal muscles would contract and spasm inside the cavern that was my stomach, while my mind spun in a psychedelic hypnotizing swirl. I'd collapse, clammy and wobbly, to the floor just outside the bathtub and pray that my brother or sister would walk by the door and hear me panting shallow requests for help to my bed. I was always waiting for someone to rescue me, while secretly hoping they wouldn't jeopardize my status as someone who always needed to be saved.

Eventually I'd crawl my way to the kitchen where I'd lie with my cheek against the cool tile, nibbling on a saltine, secure in the knowledge I had to feel only one knowable bodily pain. With such extreme physical weakness and the possibility of severe malnourishment, there was just no need to think about anything else that hurt in my life. Nothing else was as dangerous and life-threatening. The weightiness of this problem, juxtaposed against my own spectacular physical lightness, obscured the reality of my deep emotional hurt. Within this persistent suffering, I felt good at avoiding pain. It took years for me to consider that maybe if I stopped trying to control how I hurt, I'd feel a pain that would teach me what I need to do to love life more and need pain less. That maybe if I released the torture that made me feel safe, I'd wade through the discomfort of what was really bothering me so that I could live a life less defined by pain.

When we identify where we're hurting and why, whether it's something physical or emotional, we have the power to understand its cause and do something about it. But that means we have to be willing to let go of all the drama, comfort, and maybe even pride that accompany a sad story to make way for a better one. Before we can learn from our pain to make positive change in our lives, we have to learn how to want pain less. Once we decide to stop clinging to, chasing, and controlling pain, then we have immense power to shape our worlds.

We can take almost anything that hurts and recycle it into something good once we're ready to learn from it. If you're hurting over trouble in your relationship, your pain may be teaching you that you need to find the strength to walk away. If you're hurting because people don't seem to like you, your pain may be teaching you that you need to stop depending on approval for your overall well-being. If you're hurting because your thoughts are tormenting you, your pain may be teaching you that you alone are the cause of your deepest suffering, and that in accepting that, you have the power to set yourself free. Of course this all depends on the most important question: are you ready to be free?

Learn from pain to make positive changes.

If you're hurting and feeling angry, resentful, or resistant:

Identify the cause of your pain. Are you reliving something that happened long ago? Are you hurting because of a current situation that isn't working for you? It's easier to stuff pain down than to address it, but you can only learn about what you need if you're willing to acknowledge that you haven't gotten it and how that makes you feel. The next step is to ask yourself if you have some investment in hurting. Is there a part of you that wants to stay in a situation that you know is bad? You can only let go of pain if you understand why you're holding on to it.

Feel the pain. Don't try to hide it, avoid it, fight it, or run from it—sit with it instead. It may feel overwhelming, but know that every feeling eventually transforms, and it will happen faster if you stop resisting. Sink deep into it and get clear about exactly why it hurts. What is it that you want to change?

Continues

Establish what this pain teaches you to change. If you're hurting over an event from the past or something that's completely out of your hands, the only thing you have the power to change is how and when you think about that issue. That means accepting that there are some things you cannot control and deciding not to waste this moment fighting that, because this moment—right now—is all there is. If you're hurting over something in the present—like a relationship that doesn't serve you or a sense of loneliness—the pain is teaching you that you need to move on or meet new people. Once you establish the lesson, you have the power to use it. The only thing standing between you and freedom is your story about why you can't have it.

Pain helps us appreciate pleasure

Without suffering, we would never fully understand joy. **~@Sequential**

There is suffering for us to recognize the meaning of happiness. There can't be one without the other. **~@Laurie_AMU**

Others' suffering lets me give hope, charity, and love. My suffering gives these opportunities to others. No humanity without it. **~@dgalvin22**

There's suffering in the world in order to show us how much beauty there is, too. You could not have one without the other. **~@cphilli3**

Suffering brings joy, happiness, love, generosity, and all good things into relief so that we may recognize them. **~@LittleWordGods**

On the other side of our instinct to avoid pain, there's the persistent longing for things that feel good—what Sigmund Freud referred to as the pleasure principle. What's interesting to note, though, is that pain and pleasure really are intricately connected—not just because they are two sides of the same coin but also because one often creates the other. When we experience stress or pain, our bodies create endorphins that intercept the messages that would tell the brain the body should hurt. It's why a lot of people engage in thrill-seeking activities that may cause them physical discomfort, and also why athletes push through—the euphoric high that accompanies immense pain.

It's also why people eat chili peppers, which contain a high amount of capsaicin, a compound that triggers pain receptors through a burning sensation. In his 2008 *Washington Post* article "The Pleasure Is in the Pain," Andreas Viestad discusses his trip to the world's "Chili Belt," where he conducted research for a book on spices. In Mozambique, Thailand, and India, he observed a dramatic shift in energy and enthusiasm after people consumed a chili-pepper-infused meal. One of the men in Maputo explained they cry so hard while eating the spicy foods so that they can laugh after the meal.

This same idea applies in many areas of our lives. We watch tragic films to experience the cathartic release of engaging in emotional stories. We choose to watch violent murders in horror movies, even though we'd never want to see or be someone actually being maimed or tortured, because we want to feel those primal sensations of fear while knowing we're safely removed from any actual danger. We alternate dives in the icy pool with quick dips in the hot tub, enjoying dramatically shifting our body temperatures in a short amount of time. And then there's the way we take on professional and personal challenges knowing there are difficulty and risk involved. Pain paves the path for pleasure—and sometimes, as I mentioned before, we feel the greater the hurt, the sweeter the reward.

In addition to creating conditions for pleasure, pain helps us survive—which is, in fact, a prerequisite for feeling good. In his book *The Gift of Pain*, Paul Brand explores how the experience of pain helps us understand what we need to do to preserve our bodies. He references a girl who was born with congenital indifference to pain, meaning she couldn't experience any of the physical sensations we'd associate with hurting. At eighteen months old, she chewed at her fingers beyond the point of bleeding, completely oblivious to the fact that her wounded digits represented a massive threat to her well-being. Obviously adults know better than to gnaw on our own flesh, but without pain we wouldn't have information we need to preserve ourselves. This doesn't apply just to physical pain; emotional pain also helps us make smart choices for our survival.

I've always had a fascination with the idea of schadenfreude—deriving pleasure through seeing someone else in pain—because some of my most painful memories involve me crying while someone else appeared to enjoy it. A recent study by University of Chicago psychology professor Jean Decety revealed that bullies experience increased blood flow in the reward center of the brain when they see people suffering. Children who didn't display similarly aggressive behavior felt empathy for the people hurting.

Considering that biology may have influenced the cruelty I experienced as a kid—and knowing that my tormenters may have missed out on an important cue to feel for other people and, in doing so, intimately relate to them—I can feel a new and healthy gratitude for my ability to hurt. The capacity to feel for other people is in itself a source of pleasure. Because I hurt so deeply, I have always felt other people's pain almost within my own flesh and blood. I may not always have opened myself up to relationships, but I've always been a nurturer within the ones I've accepted. For that deeply satisfying ability to recognize pain and help heal it, I am eternally grateful.

The pleasure that can come after pain isn't always a reciprocal or fair trade-off, but if we have to experience things that are difficult in life, we might as well identify something good in the aftermath. When I met that girl in Times Square, I knew without a doubt she would never have chosen her fate. There was nothing desirable about losing the people she loved and knowing they died so tragically. It crossed my mind, though, that she likely appreciated people in a whole new way after experiencing firsthand just how fragile life is. I imagined that in her next relationship, whenever things got difficult, as they inevitably do when two people come together, she'd close her eyes and remember to value every moment because the moments eventually run out. Knowing the pain of loss likely gave her relationships a whole new sense of meaning.

At the end of his life, French impressionist painter Auguste Renoir continued making art, despite the near-paralyzing arthritis that made every stroke torture. In response to the question of why he carried on, Renoir said, "Pain passes but beauty remains." I can't help but wonder if he didn't merely push through the pain but somehow appreciated that it endowed his last pieces with a whole new sense of meaning. Pain has a way of doing that when we realize what we get through the experience of enduring it.

Let pain remind you of what you enjoy and appreciate.

If you're hurting and it seems like you'll never feel joy again:

Identify what this pain reminds you to appreciate. If you're hurting because you lost someone, this pain reminds you to enjoy every moment with the people you love because life is fragile. If you're hurting because of shame or regret, this pain reminds you to live with honor, authenticity, and integrity to create feelings of self-respect and pride.

Make a proactive decision to enjoy those things at least a little today. Don't worry about completely releasing your pain forever—that's a huge goal to demand of yourself. Instead, focus on doing something for just a short while that will create the emotions you want to feel. Call an old friend and get together for a spontaneous adventure instead of dwelling on the adventure that never happened. Do something that makes you feel proud and passionate instead of feeling ashamed of the decision that didn't pan out.

Schedule blocks of healing. When we're hurting, it's easy to isolate ourselves until we feel better or more in control. But I've noticed that simple pleasures—like a massage or a hug—can feel so much more gratifying when I am deeply in need of release or connection. So schedule it in, even if you think you may get emotional. According to William Frey II, a biochemist who researches tears at Ramsey Medical Center, crying releases toxins and stress hormones—meaning, it often feels good to cry.

Desires and attachment cause pain

Because there is desire, there is suffering. ~@jazzmann91

Suffering happens when people become attached to material possessions
and each other. Understanding loss and death will free us. ~@lindsay1657

People identify with every thought they have. They don't see the world as it is.
They just see their opinions about it. ~@mullet3000

Because we're human and have intelligence, we can imagine having a better
experience than the present and suffer over the difference. ~@sarabronfman

The day people start lowering their expectations from work, life, and
relationships, suffering will disappear. ~@supriyaagarwal

There is little in life that's more stressful than clinging to
something you want to last forever while knowing full well
that nothing does. Only slightly more painful is identifying
something you think you need and feeling powerless to get
it. There's this dream I used to have over and over again.
I'd want to get somewhere, but my body wouldn't move. I'd
start running, but I would essentially be jogging in place,
like Wile E. Coyote, legs still moving even after he'd been
pushed off the cliff and was suspended in midair. No matter
how much energy I expelled, I was immobile, but I always

kept fighting, sweating, and screaming, hoping something or someone would save me from the pain of my paralysis.

That's how I lived my waking life, too. There was always something I visualized as the end-all-be-all in terms of happiness, and it was always something that evaded me—a relationship, a job, an adventure, and usually underneath it all, a feeling. What I desperately wanted was always something just out of reach—and then I got it, and my internal supervisor immediately assigned me another aching, endless want. There was no reward for achieving—only a new demand to cower before. I suspect a lot of us live this way: desperate to be in that place where everything appears to be better. Whether it's come and gone, or it lives in a dream, we all have an idea of the way things should be. We've all formed opinions and expectations of how things look when they work well—or how we feel when things are going well. And then we attach to those situations, places, people, and feelings, imagining everything would be perfect if we could get and keep them. The irony is that we don't only attach to things that appear to be positive. Sometimes familiarly bearable is far less scary than the unknown.

Back in my adolescent group-therapy-hopping days, I met an overeater who had formed a long-term intimate relationship with a razor. She weighed more than three hundred pounds, yet even on the hottest days she wore full-length shirts—and it had nothing to do with concealing her obviously large arms. One day the therapist let us know she'd be coming to the group wearing a short-sleeved shirt. I immediately felt appalled that a professional would feel the need to prepare us for seeing an arm far fleshier than our own. Malnourished though we were, I highly doubted any of us would have gasped at the sight of her exposed obese limbs.

What I learned when I stopped thinking and tuned in to the rest of her forewarning was that our group member had cut literally hundreds of crisscrossed gashes across every inch of exposed skin she could reach. Even after years of counseling, she remained attached to this dangerous habit for numbing her emotional pain.

Months later, I learned that even our therapist felt attached to her pain. She was going through a messy divorce that she vehemently opposed even though her husband had a history of beating her. Attachment is an equal-opportunity instinct and often ignores all reason.

> **T**he moment we decide things don't have to be a certain way, we create the possibility that they could be better than we know to imagine them. **"**

Another interesting thing about attachment is that even when our target appears to be positive, sometimes it's a detrimental and limiting choice. We often attach to things we think we need without realizing the feelings they evoke aren't specific to those things. Love doesn't exist only in one relationship. Fulfillment doesn't require a specific job. Happiness doesn't depend on re-creating a past condition. Security doesn't hinge upon controlling the future and shaping it exactly as we visualize. Our grandmothers may also have advised that, often, the best things in life take us completely by surprise. As the Dalai Lama said, "Sometimes not getting what you want is a wonderful stroke of luck." One of the most popular posts on *TinyBuddha.com* is fewer than one hundred words but has received more than eleven thousand Stumbles. It reads:

> *Opportunity often hides in the most unlikely places, but it isn't easy to see it when you're disappointed life didn't meet your expectations. Michael Jordan's high school coach cut him from the basketball team, which may have pushed him to work harder and become an NBA superstar. Soichiro Honda wanted to be an engineer at Toyota until he was rejected, inspiring him to start his own company. You never know when a disappointment might pave the path for something great. What wonderful stroke of luck have you had lately, and what can you do to benefit from it?*

I suspect this one struck a nerve with people because it rarely feels safe to detach from a want, and yet some of the best things in life come from choosing to let go. The moment we decide things don't have to be a certain way, we create the possibility that they could be better than we know to imagine them. That doesn't mean we shouldn't want things; it just means we can experience a lot more joy if we learn to want without fearing. It *is* possible to visualize a goal and work toward it, and simultaneously know that even if it doesn't pan out, we can still experience happiness. Attachment is assuming we know precisely what has to happen for life to become and stay good. Detachment is a commitment to strive and then accept that, whatever happens, we can make it good. One resists the undeniable reality that life is uncontrollable and everything within it impermanent; the other gives us the permission to flourish even as we know those things are true.

Turn the pain of wanting
into the joy of doing.

If you're hurting over something you think you need and can't have:

Identify what it is you're grasping at. Is it a job that you think will make you feel passionate about your work? Is it a relationship that you feel you need in order to know love? Now ask yourself: are you assuming happiness exists in achieving or getting this specific thing? Realize that this—the belief that you will be happy only if you only get what you want—is an illusion. It's something that allows you to release responsibility for being happy right now, because "someday" everything will line up just right. That day may never come. Happiness isn't getting everything you want. It's appreciating what you have and staying open to the limitless possibilities before you.

Focus on the process, not the outcome. There's nothing wrong with striving for a specific goal; it's suffocating it with need and stress that hurts you. Instead of fixating on the outcome you want to create, focus on joy in the process. For example, with TinyBuddha, I have never known for sure where this is leading or how many people will read. But I love writing about these topics and engaging with people about letting go and letting peace in. When you focus on joy in the process, you're more likely to create and sustain momentum and positive results.

Find ways to get what you really want today, as it is. Underneath the specific goals or desires, there's a more general need. Identify that. If you want to feel passionate, do something today to indulge your passion. Volunteer your service to or barter with others, offering your skills in exchange for theirs. If you want to feel loved, start by giving love. Call a family member or get together with friends to do something you love. Sometimes when you let go of restrictive wants, you can better meet your actual needs.

We can heal each other's pain

Suffering has a place only in a world where there is insufficient empathy.
~@malengine

People have their faith put in imagination, not into other people. We need people loving each other. ~@Hey_Pato

There is immense suffering in this world because people fail to be proactive with their words and actions. ~@SkyIsOpen

The world has not yet understood that even if there are 6,861,638,344 individuals, we all make one. ~@witchy_di

A harder question is: What are you doing to alleviate the suffering?
~@UncleElvis

It's clear that pain is necessary, though suffering can be avoided. This might seem to imply that we alone hold the responsibility for minimizing our anguish. If we have trouble doing this, the next logical conclusion is that we should hide it and bear it alone. A lot of us learned growing up that strength means not showing emotion, and definitely not admitting vulnerability. This doesn't actually convince anyone that we don't hurt and we aren't vulnerable, because everyone with a pulse does and is.

We can't avoid hurting in life, and if we did, it would be dangerous. Pain tells us we're alive. Pain challenges us, guides us, and connects us. Everyone feels the same things in life, though at different times and in different ways. Even if no one else has dealt with the specific challenge you face— and that is unlikely—everyone else has felt the same overwhelming sense of confusion, fear, and terror. Regardless of how distressing the details of your past may be, someone else can relate to the exact feelings of disappointment, disillusionment, and anger. Someone might look completely confident and together, but be sure that at some point, he's felt insecure and scared. Another may appear to be bold and fulfilled, but know that, in the distant or very recent past, she's closed the blinds, burrowed under the covers, and exhausted herself through gut-wrenching tears.

Pain is not a sign of weakness, but bearing it alone is a choice to grow weak. It's only in finding the courage to admit our pain that we can lean on each other. And why shouldn't we? Knowing that we all go through the same things and that most people *do* feel compassion for each other, why should we shroud ourselves in shame simply for being human?

> **B**eing disliked and misunderstood by some is worth the freedom of knowing you are loved and supported by many. "

In 2012, several teen suicides made headlines, shining a light on the dangers of bullying, particularly in our always-on, Internet-enabled world. Knowing firsthand how easy it is to hate yourself when you believe that everyone else does too, I can only imagine the horror of having the harassment extend to Facebook, online chats, and text messages. In the aftermath of these tragedies, writer Dan Savage and his partner posted a video of compassion and hope online. A whole campaign, It Gets Better, grew naturally from that. In a number of simple yet powerful videos, celebrities and those less well known stare straight at the screen and, one by one, with kind eyes and implied understanding, remind the viewer that no matter how hard things may seem, "It gets better." It's easy to disbelieve, since we can never know for certain what the future holds, but most of us have experienced some type of transformative pain in our lives. If we're still alive, it likely *has* gotten better—if not in every way, in some.

As I watched these videos, imagining how therapeutic they would have been to twelve-year-old me, when I seriously considered all avenues to end my despair, something occurred to me: What if we all extended that same compassion far before others got to the point where they life-or-death needed it? What if we opened our eyes and recognized the small signs that someone's hurting and then let her know we've been there, too, and we'll be there for her now?

Of course, it's not just the outsiders who have a responsibility. All the support in the world will be useless if those who are hurting refuse to admit we need it. In an article about Phoebe Prince, one of the bullied teenagers who committed suicide, Emily Bazelon cited a definition of bullying as "repeated acts of abuse that involve a power imbalance." By this definition, it seems clear to me that a lot of us bully ourselves. We choose to take away our own power by beating ourselves up even further than did the external injury. We torment ourselves in silence to avoid feeling vulnerable and inferior.

Of all the burdens I've carried around, the heaviest was the belief that I was wrong to be hurting—that enlightened people felt pain like a raindrop on their shoe whereas I let it hit me like a self-contained tsunami because I was tragically weak. I felt certain I had to either hide or package myself in smiles and lies—otherwise I'd expose the ugliest flaw in my character. I've come to realize that the only mistake when it comes to pain is to assume life shouldn't involve it and that pain often starts to dull when I decide to embrace it, acknowledge it, and grow from it. Sadness, fear, disgust, and even anger can make the world a better place if we find the strength to channel them toward something good.

Why is there suffering the world? Because there is—the more important question is: what good can we do for ourselves and each other, knowing that pain to be inevitable?

Let your pain connect you to other people.

Instead of sitting alone in your pain:

Be honest with other people about what you're experiencing. Nothing feels more liberating than the freedom to be exactly where you are, without apologizing or trying to protect yourself from judgment. That doesn't mean that no will judge you—some people will, and that's just life. Be honest anyway. Being disliked and misunderstood by some is worth the freedom of knowing you are loved and supported by many.

Express yourself to release the feelings, not to dwell on them. There's a difference between sharing your experiences for support and seeking an audience with no intention of finding a solution. Whether you're talking to your friends or to strangers in a support group, be honest about your experience but release the need to pull them into the story. Your goal isn't to create an identity so that people constantly relate to your pain; it's to share your pain so that you can release it, allowing people the opportunity to relate to all of you.

Help heal other people's pain. Because you know what pain feels like, you can recognize it in other people—so be there in the way you'd want it. For me, that means asking, "How can I help?" when someone seems burdened, and then being open to whatever is needed without judgment or expectation; or giving someone an uncomfortably long hug when he appears to be weak, allowing him to melt into my arms. We are all in this together. Now we just have to act like it.

MEANING

WHAT'S THE
MEANING OF LIFE?

~~~~~~~~~~~~~~~~~~~~~~~~~~~~~

It's perhaps the oldest and most frequently asked question in the world: why are we all here? The persistent need to make sense of life, to gain some semblance of control in an otherwise uncertain world, is one of the few things that unites us all. No matter how much we gain or how much we learn, there's no escaping the reality that nothing is permanent and a lot is unknowable.

To temper our uneasiness about what we might lose, how we might hurt, and how desperately we want to believe there's some reason for it all, we cling to ideas of what it all might mean—what the events of our lives mean about the grand picture, what our accomplishments mean about us, what we mean to the people we meet, and what our lives mean in the context of history. We can never know for sure what life itself means, but we can know that *we* mean something in a potentially meaningless world. When we realize that our actions might be our only hope at living a meaningful life, it's easy to feel paralyzed. After all, purpose is something deliberate, something grand, something beautiful—something people would want to talk about. Meaning can be a high-pressure situation if we don't trust ourselves to identify it and then live in accordance with it.

At twenty-four years old, I'd officially set up shop in Manhattan, where I planned to become a Broadway star. I was rarely sure I liked myself, but I was certain I loved myself when I gutted myself onstage and filled the hole with a fictional character. Also: everyone else knew that I came to New York to become someone. I felt desperate to succeed on a massive scale—to take that small bit of joy I felt while in a costume and pump it into an aura of greatness that everyone could see, admire, and respect.

Going to New York was easy; doing something when I got there, not so much. If I pursued my purpose and failed, I'd have to acknowledge that I wasn't good enough to do what I was meant to do, and worse yet, I'd confirm what I assumed to be my family members' suspicions: that I was inadequate and a horrible disappointment. You could have watched me from afar for a lifetime and never have known it, but you'd have been certain if you looked into my eyes for even a second: for the vast majority of my life, I believed the words *Lori Deschene* meant "worthless." In fear of confirming this under a magnifying spotlight, I tucked myself into a hole of a home the moment I got to New York. If I chose to sit on the sidelines, I figured, I wasn't choosing not to try; I was just waiting for the right time.

I worked for four hours a day as a telemarketer and lived in a week-to-week single-room-occupancy building, somewhat like a dorm for crackheads, prostitutes, and little girls lost. On most afternoons, after work, I filled a small rolling suitcase with the necessities I didn't want stolen if someone ransacked my place for drug money and then made the trek to the Times Square Internet Café. After finding a relatively odorless spot to camp out through the evening, I'd dive into Craigslist, hoping to emerge at the surface of reality with some answer as to what I should do and who I should be. I looked for jobs; I searched for roommate situations; I browsed the event section to fantasize about hobbies I might take up; I even frequented the platonic personals section for friendships. Although I made a few peripheral connections, I knew I wasn't going to really open myself up to new people and experiences. It was like I was creating a vision board for a life I had no intention of realizing in the foreseeable future. I was pretty much just going through the motions. I was "trying" to fill my life, while secretly feeling opposed to the risk it would involve.

One month into my daily web surfing, I met Rich and Jim, two middle-aged homeless men who looked more like suburbanites who'd simply been car-sprayed with a muddy rain puddle. Rich and Jim owned an online software-support company that went bankrupt after 9/11. Having put all their funding and energy into the business, they decided to go for broke—to stay in NYC despite their dwindling resources and to sacrifice everything for their goals, including their rent money. When I met them, they were thousands in the hole, with holes throughout their newspaper-lined coats, and close to having their servers shut down. Yet I never got any sense of anger or despondency from them. They were like cocky kids going for their black belts, each sparring against the best at the dojo—even massive bruises and bloody welts would be cool if they came with victory and bragging rights.

I immediately wanted to be like them. I imagined what it would feel like to package all of the events in my life as signs that I was on the right track, even when presented with abundant evidence to the contrary. I wondered how liberating it would feel to do only what I really wanted to do and to ostracize myself out of passion instead of fear. I ached for that sense of blind faith and obliviousness and hoped perhaps they'd give it to me, like a communicable disease they caught on the street. I wanted to gather everyone else's expectations and use them as fuel for a trash-can fire that would warm our odd little threesome.

Rich and Jim were my first friends in NYC, and after several months and hundreds of heart-opening conversations, I trusted them implicitly. One cold, bitter night as I was leaving the café, I heard Rich tell Jim the shelter was full. They'd put in yet another twelve-hour workday, and now they'd need to cuddle on a park bench and hope to avoid frostbite, pneumonia, and police harassment. My mouth knew what this meant before my brain formulated a thought: "I have some room," I said aloud. By *some* I meant a four-by-six patch of floor, the only extra space, right next to my bed.

I knew I hardly knew them, but that same logic hadn't seemed to stop me from being alone with myself. For two weeks they shared my shoebox room, squished together on an air mattress like two oversize, mismatched spoons. They'd leave early in the morning, head to their storage space for clothes, and then go to the café to work on a deal. They were always "so close" to closing a deal. One day, after multiple late-payment warnings, their servers went down. All they'd sacrificed, all the cold nights they'd spent on the street, all the work they'd put in—gone, leaving them with nothing to show for their loyalty to possibility.

And I still had nothing but the hope of seeing them succeed. All the space another person might fill with her own ambition I overflowed with voyeuristic support for Rich and Jim. If I couldn't champion their comeback story and ride their rags-to-riches coattails as the one who believed in them, what I feared was reality would actually be true: my life meant nothing because I was doing nothing. With far more desperation than I registered, I pulled out my credit card and fronted them $700. They had to keep going. I had to hold on to their dream.

If my life were a movie, the next part would be the montage that's often referred to as "fun and games" in the film industry. You'd see them high-fiving at the computer as business appears to increase exponentially. You'd catch a glimpse of us doing a three-way *Laverne & Shirley* schlemiel-schlimazel in unified elation over everything that's going right. As a viewer, you'd know I made the right choice—that my risk paid off, and they were well on their way to creating a money-making, history-breaking venture. And then the impact would hit as strong as a frozen anvil to the face when you saw me standing alone in my room, the $100 in cash I kept hidden under my bed gone, and Rich and Jim no more than the dirty air mattress they popped before they left.

In one fell swoop, I lost my only friends and the illusion that I was living a life that meant something. How could I have been so naïve and pathetic? In a prolonged dramatic gesture, I walked over to the mirror, stared deeply into my empty eyes—murmuring that I was stupid, hopeless, and worthless—and then, putting all my anger into a forceful grab, shattered the mirror against the floor, the shards scattering all along the deflated bed.

I would sooner have slumped there forever, alone with shame and sorrow, than risk going into the world and proving beyond a shadow of a doubt that I meant nothing. Not that my life meant nothing—that *I* did. If you opened the dictionary to *Lori Deschene*, I feared, you'd wonder how a single piece of paper could express such a putrid-smelling, soul-sucking emptiness.

When I was younger, I used to say words repeatedly to wear them down, a lot like tossing food in the blender and completely forgetting it had once been a solid item. I'd start while I was coloring or doing some other solitary activity, murmuring, "Refrigerator. Refrigerator. Refriiiigeeeeraaatooor." If I said it often enough, suddenly I began to forget what exactly it meant. It would even start to sound foreign, made up, empty—like a balloon suddenly losing its air. As I sat there staring at the broken glass, trying to numb myself against the indignity of my fearful choices, I found myself muttering, "Lori Deschene," wondering what other people thought when they said it.

I started slowly and softly, as if trying to whisper into my own ear, hoping to reach my spirit without jarring it. I watched the multiple pieces of my mouth scattered in glass along the floor. Then I hastened the pace a little, trying to make the words become unfamiliar. I mumbled them over and over again, tripping on them, spitting them out, trying desperately to forget what they meant—to forget that I'd decided years ago how little that name could ever mean. And then I fell asleep, wondering if I'd ever look in the mirror and like what I saw.

I didn't strip away any layers of myself that night, but slammed so low, I began to learn something that has shaped and guided every day that's followed since: emptiness can be a horrible or wonderful thing, depending on where it comes from. You can wallow in misery, feeling like you have nothing to offer the world just because you haven't figured it out yet. Or you can feel a sense of emptiness that's at once terrifying and liberating, because it means you've let go of who you've been and have opened up to who you can be. It's the deep and dark cavern of possibility and light. It's freedom from what the past has meant and what the future might mean, and it's a sense that now can mean anything.

Emily Dickinson wrote, "To live is so startling it leaves time for little else." I've often wondered if it's possible to live this fully—if anyone can feel so in awe of the experience of her daily life that she simply doesn't have time to hurt over yesterday, worry about tomorrow, and be consumed with theories as to what it all means and what her life *should* mean. Just the other day, I read about a research study from Washington University and the University of Arizona that showed people who tackle the pithy topics have a stronger sense of well-being than people who keep things superficial. What this tells me is that we can't ignore our human instinct to want more. We can't pretend there's literally no room for something else. There *is*—there's lots of room. Life leaves plenty of time for solitude and contemplation. Even busy people have time and space to fill, if not in their schedules, in their minds. The beautiful part of life is that regardless of what it means, we can share the puzzle together. We don't have to sit alone in emptiness. Just by engaging with each other, we can transform hollow bewilderment into full-frontal wonder.

With that in mind, I asked on Twitter, "What's the meaning of life?"

The meaning of life is to live every day fully and enjoy it

Life is not the pursuit of happiness. It's the happiness in your pursuits.
~@ac_awesome

The meaning of life is to live life and experience this world to the fullest, from dark to light and everything in between. ~@Jay_Rey

Life is about learning, sharing, never giving up, and having fun.
~@ lida4ibu

The meaning of life is to become truly happy and to live each day based on courage and compassion. ~@puffinclaire

Life's meaning is to be open to all that comes your way and to pursue whatever your heart desires. ~@mmalbrecht

Occam's razor states that the simplest answer is usually the right one, but humans don't do so well with simple. We like to identify patterns in our lives so that we can think about what we think it all means. We get so fixated on why specific past events occurred and what we can do to make specific future events occur that we often miss being in the occurrences of now. It's not easy to accept that what is just is. We want stories—a story explaining how we got here; a story guiding the day as it happens, like the ever-wise, ever-calm voice-overs you hear in the movies; and a story to leave behind when we pass on so our lives will mean something more than the simple, solo experiences of living them.

It's not nearly satisfying enough if the point of life is to live each moment fully, because that doesn't provide an answer as to why the moments eventually run out. A moment will never seem like enough when you pit it against the desire for an endless supply of moments. In Will Durant's *On the Meaning of Life*, a compilation of perspectives from Depression-era luminaries, Sinclair Lewis explored the irrelevance of mortality and religion to our everyday enjoyment. He wrote, "If I go to a play I do not enjoy it less because I do not believe that it is divinely created and divinely conducted, that it will last forever instead of stopping at eleven, that many details of it will remain in my memory after a few months, or that it will have any particular moral effect upon me. And I enjoy life as I enjoy that play."

I suspect it's hard to adopt this philosophy and focus on the show we're at because we know intellectually that there are an infinite number of other plays we could be at; but because of the limitations of time, we can't possibly see all of them. And then there's the reality that each play has a price, and you have obligations to fill outside the theater and anxieties about them that might drown out the encore.

Enjoyment isn't solely dependent on our determination to make peace with the big things we don't know; it hinges on our ability to forget for a while all the little things we do know—the circumstances of our lives and the inevitability of struggle on the other side of fun. Even if enjoyment is the meaning of life, it's simply not possible to enjoy every moment. Does that render the unenjoyable moments meaningless?

A friend of mine once told me that fun is the meaning of life. He's the closest to a real-life Forrest Gump I've ever met. Because he loves music, he devoted himself to his radio job and eventually worked his way up to station manager. He spends most weekends surfing, going to concerts, trying different adventures, and roaming through his childlike existence with a sense of delight and wonder. Because he believes that fun is the ultimate point of it all, he measures everything against that barometer. If it isn't fun for him, he doesn't do it; if it is fun, he does it often. This declaration seemed far too simple from my vantage point, and certainly not an effective way to be sure it all leads somewhere good.

I've spent a lot of time through the years watching this friend, like he's a theory I want to poke holes in. I could not fathom that enjoyment could be a fulfilling purpose in and of itself. There's abundant research showing that people with a sense of individual meaning feel happier than do people who see actions as random and inconsequential. If we don't believe we have a strong driving motivation, what will push us through the moments that *aren't* fun?

Then I noticed something about my friend: he has difficult times like the rest of us, but when they hit, instead of sitting around dwelling on what it all means, he goes out and does the things that make him feel meaningful. He doesn't enjoy everything in life, but he chooses more often than not to do the things he enjoys, and in doing so feels fulfilled.

Perhaps enjoyment is *a* meaning of life, but only as a consequence of our doing what feels meaningful to us. By choosing to do the things we love, we shift the balance of empty moments to complete ones. When we're focused on creating and enjoying fun—immersing ourselves in the various "whats" that get us excited—suddenly it seems less important to understand the one ultimate "why."

Create meaning through joy.

If you've gotten a little too serious in your pursuit of purpose:

Make a list of three to seven things that you enjoy most in life. These don't have to be huge things. They might be simple things, like walking on the beach, riding your motorcycle, or listening to the sound of your baby laughing. Think about the activities that often leave you thinking, *This is what it means to really be alive.*

Take a look at your current schedule. Do you regularly do those things? Are you making excuses about why you can't? Maybe it's your busy schedule, or your limited finances, or some other external restriction.

Find tiny holes in your upcoming week. Even if you're busy, odds are you have an hour here, twenty minutes there, and maybe even a complete day or two sometimes. Identify potential gaps right now, acknowledging that they're available to be filled.

Plan to do something that makes you feel exhilarated for at least a small chunk of time every day. If you love animals but don't ever spend time with them, go to a local dog park during your lunch break. If you're passionate about yoga but can't afford a class, find a free one on YouTube. Plan for a little activity every day that makes you feel alive and connected to something larger than yourself—even if it's for just fifteen minutes. Then do only those things, without carrying your worries or fears into the moment. When you make time to experience pure, engaged joy, you both create meaning and open to new possibilities that may create more.

The meaning of life is to make a difference in the world

Leave the world at least a little bit better than you found it. ~@ealcantara

Serve as an example. ~@amadeoatthesun

I think the meaning of life is creation. ~@Auraxx

Life is to live, not just to survive; for the self to express itself; to know the self, the supreme self, and to serve others. ~@wupendram

Have it matter that you lived. ~@RAZE502

There's this saying I used to love that doesn't resonate with me anymore: go big or go home.

I understand the allure of doing big things with a massive audience watching. It's kind of like the whole tree-in-the-woods analogy. If you live a beautiful life and no one remembers it, did it even happen at all? It's why we carve our names into trees and bury time capsules. We want a sense that even if our lives are limited by time, the memories of what we contributed to society will far outlast our own drop-in-the-bucket life span. It's an extension of our survival instincts: the drive to live on at all costs, even in spite of our inevitable deaths, and to aid in the progress of future generations, ensuring that they inherit a better world than the one we knew.

If purpose is a gateway to happiness, and happiness is inevitably impermanent, as all feelings are, we can easily ascertain during the unhappy moments that our purpose isn't good enough or else it would provide more lasting positive feelings. Worrying about whether our purpose is big, or worthy, enough can completely strip the joy from living in alignment with our purpose.

As I was searching for different perspectives on the meaning of life, I found a number of books that sought answers from highly public, influential people. There was the Durant book I mentioned before. Next there was *The Meaning of Life: Wisdom, Humor, and Damn Good Advice from 64 Extraordinary Lives*, compiled by *Esquire* editor Ryan D'Agostino. Then there was *Vanity Fair's Proust Questionnaire: 101 Luminaries Ponder Love, Death, Happiness, and the Meaning of Life*. The implication seems to be that extraordinary accomplishment somehow endows someone with a sense of authority as to what matters the most in life.

When I mentioned this to my boyfriend, Ehren, he commented that we also enjoy stories that show good average people finding meaning within their circumstances. As I write this, it's almost Christmas, and I've dreamed of lassoing the moon two nights in a row in anticipation of soon watching *It's a Wonderful Life*. Still, I can't help noticing that movies based on real events rarely feature truly ordinary people. The Patch Adamses, Erin Brockoviches, and Frank Abagnales of the world make for more compelling stories than do the real-life George Baileys. It's almost like we've decided a life is more valuable if its story somehow sticks out from all the others.

My grandfather spent a great deal of his life working as a maintenance man. Although he died more than fifteen years ago, his name lives on. Grampy coached baseball for both of my uncles' childhood teams, focusing on fairness above all else. He had forty-four kids under his supervision, so he split them into four teams and rotated through them all in every game. Kids who didn't get to play any innings were the first ones to play next time, regardless of their skill. They rarely ever won, but Grampy didn't care about that. Some coaches bought their kids ice cream only after a victory. My grandfather did it whenever he could afford to, because he didn't think their fun should hinge on how skillfully they played the game. My grandmother still runs into Grampy's former players who to this day appreciate his kindness, thoughtfulness, and generosity.

When Grampy was fifty-five, he lost both of his legs to a staph infection he contracted while in the hospital for bypass surgery. He could easily have gotten bitter about the unfairness of it all, but I don't remember him ever stewing in anger or self-pity—not even after the infection spread from the first to the second leg. He'd already retired at that point and because his legs were now amputated above the knees, he became permanently confined to a wheelchair. Still, he sat center stage at every community theater rehearsal and even helped my group get on the local news by pitching our play to the entertainment reporter. Our director nominated Grampy for the Channel 56 Independent Spirit award, which honors people who have done outstanding work for their communities.

As Grampy sat at the award ceremony, both tiny and massive in his chair, cradling that award, I suspected that what really mattered to him was that he'd lived a life he was proud of. That's what I remember when my efforts seem small—that the biggest reward is sitting peacefully in the knowledge that I'm being the person I want to be. We do humanity a disservice if we believe we all, universally, need to meet some preconceived expectation of *big* in order to be living meaningful lives. What *really* fulfills us is a sense that we're using our time in a way that aligns with our own instincts and values—that we're making the difference we want to make in the way we want to make it.

We can live our lives struggling to change the world—we can try to do important things before anyone else or hard things better than everyone else. That's one way to go about it, and it's a perfectly valid approach. We can live our lives struggling to change the world—we can try to do important things before anyone else or hard things better than anyone else. That's one way to go about it, and it's a perfectly valid approach. But that's not the only way to make a difference. We get to choose what's meaningful and impactful and how we go about accomplishing it. There aren't any right or wrong answers as long as we choose the answers for ourselves, based on what we actually believe matters. At the end of it all, what flashes before our eyes won't be all the things we did that were bigger than ourselves; they'll be all the moments when we made a difference by being true to ourselves.

Make the difference you want to make today.

If you're not sure you're making a difference in the world:

Identify what makes you feel proud of yourself. Or, put another way: what would you feel good about giving back to the world? This doesn't need to be an all-encompassing purpose that carries you through the rest of your life. Think in terms of what feels right in this moment. If you were to die tomorrow, what would you want people to remember of you? For example, if tomorrow were my last day, I'd want people to remember me as someone who helped people hurt less and enjoy more.

Recognize the percentage of time you spend striving for meaning. If your day is a pie chart, what percentage do you devote to striving, plotting, planning, and struggling toward a point in the future when you feel you'll be able to live your purpose? How much time, exactly, do you spend postponing meaning until some point in the future when you become more successful or impactful?

Choose to balance the equation. Today is all you're guaranteed, which means today is not just one stone along the path to making a big difference *someday*; it's also the opportunity to make small differences right now. You do that by making tiny choices that align with the lofty goal. You might not be a published self-help writer yet, but you can assist one person today by listening. You may not have made your documentary on families yet, but you can get your own family together tonight and embody the values you want to explore on film. Whatever you want to do on a big scale, shrink it and do it right now. You may not yet have the impact you think you need, but there's a lot you can do within your sphere of influence that still makes a difference.

Love is the meaning of life

The meaning of life is making connections with other people. Think about it: things are always best when shared. ~@krillhei

Kindness is the meaning of life. It says I want you to be happy. There are no hidden motives. ~@Scilixx

Simply put, the meaning of life is to live. Life is found in our everyday interactions, kindness, and love for others. ~@JoshMPlant

The meaning of life is to create and love all life. ~@Jon_Maynell

The meaning of life is to radiate and reflect back the selfless love and compassion that emanates from a loved one to the entire world around you. ~@smokyogi

If pop culture has taught us anything, it's that all we need is love, but we aren't quite sure what it is. When I was younger, I thought love was literally magic. I imagined it as a luminescence, something that could embrace two people in some type of protective, light-drenched cocoon. At five years old, this made perfect sense to me—that when two people love each other, their hearts synchronize and transform together into something bigger and infinitely more powerful than anything else that has ever or could ever exist.

I believed fully in that magic and, unlike my supposedly undying devotion to the ideas of Santa Claus and the Easter Bunny, that ideal never fully faded as I grew older. Even after I learned that some adults divorce and get nasty with each other, or stay married and berate each other, and long after I understood that some people create new people without even liking each other, I still believed transformative, all-encompassing love was the closest thing to real magic that we can ever know in this lifetime. I thought love would one day crack open my world, shake out everything that hurt, and heal it all under the light of unconditional acceptance and affection.

I didn't realize it back then, but I was fantasizing about an escape from the pain of being me—and the nearest exit I could imagine was someone, *anyone*, else. But a lot of the people I clung to were anything but loving toward me. It's easy to confuse attachment with love, particularly when we consider that we come into this world and leave it alone—that we are part of the whole but still apart. So, is it possible to ascertain the love that is the meaning of life? Can an obscure, moving, and eventually disintegrating target really be the point of it all?

In his book *Man's Search for Meaning*, Austrian psychiatrist and Holocaust survivor Viktor Frankl explored his three years at Dachau, Auschwitz, and other concentration camps. Surrounded by death and depravity, with every reason to grow bitter, resentful, and resigned, Frankl decided that people can endure anything if they have a compelling reason to do so. One of his driving motivations was to see his imprisoned pregnant wife again. He'd think about her smile, her presence, and the reunion they'd have when they could finally be together again. His love for her helped him endure dehumanization, disillusionment, and immense suffering. Frankl lived in a constant state of torturous uncertainty— about when his number might be called and about whether his wife's already had been—but his longing gave him a purpose—to push through for her and their life together.

Based on this understanding, you might assume that he lost the will to live when he finally walked out a free man and learned his wife and most of the rest of his family had been killed. If his love for them kept him going, their being gone should have meant he stopped. Instead, he knew the power of love to continually provide meaning, even after a loved one has passed.

Frankl recounts a conversation he had with another man who lost his wife. Having cherished her as the most important thing in his world, the widower felt crippled and severely depressed in her absence. Frankl asked what might have happened if *he* had died first, leaving her to mourn his loss. When the widower realized the turn of events saved her the agony of grieving over him, he appeared to adopt a whole new perspective on the experience of living without her—perhaps because it had some meaning. His suffering prevented hers. He could stay strong and purposeful, even without her, by focusing more on what love expected from him than on what he expected from love.

Most of us don't need to hold on to love to push us through agonizingly tragic circumstances. A great deal of what we consider unbearable is really just highly unpleasant, at worst. But just because we don't need the full power of love doesn't mean we can't benefit from it: love isn't just something we want to secure for ourselves—it's something that can help pull us outside of ourselves. I know that I've felt my lowest and emptiest often when I was drowning in my own self-involvement—all the things I thought I needed and my immense frustration over how unlikely it seemed that I would ever get them.

Most of them weren't even slightly important in the grand scheme of things. And bemoaning how I didn't have them just distracted me from appreciating all the things I did have—those little things Frankl dreamed about when he was pushing toward his uncertain future: meaningful relationships, the freedom to enjoy them, and the power to make a positive difference in other people's lives. No matter the event, it can become meaningful if it somehow helps other people. All we need *is* love, but not as something we wait to receive—as something we repeatedly make and share.

Find meaning through shared love.

If you feel like you aren't finding the love that you seek:

Identify who you can help because of what you've experienced. Are you more insightful because of your struggles, enabling you to be more sensitive to other people? Can you write a blog post or an article to help people at large? We are all in this together, and everything that happens to one person ripples to affect others. If whatever happened hasn't affected you in a positive way, how can you filter that through your love so that it can be a positive for other people?

Focus on what other people mean to you and what you want to mean to them. If this were your last day on Earth, what would you tell the people you love about what they've meant to you? Now, actually tell them today. What difference would you want them to feel you've made in their lives? Would you want them to feel you helped encourage them to go after their dreams? Or motivated them to be good to themselves? Or helped them discover their purpose? What can you do today to create that impact in their lives?

Do something kind for someone you don't know. It might be something small, like holding a door open, or it could be something bigger, like asking a homeless person if there's someone you can call for them. Sometimes we forget that we are part of something much larger than ourselves, but we are always profoundly comforted while doing something that reminds us there's a bigger picture and we're part of it.

Our purpose is to learn and grow

Life's about learning that there are always constraints and learning to be happy with, not in spite of them. ~@**objo**

Life is a journey that is a learning experience for each soul. The day we stop learning we stop living. ~@**kumudinni**

Science defines living things by growth and response to stimuli. Hence, meaning of life: to grow in response to circumstances. ~@**clairemoments**

The meaning of life is to grow and learn from each moment—to feel it, take a lesson, and improve yourself. ~@**saumya6**

The meaning of life is to evolve and connect. Learn and adapt and share it. ~@**lindsayquinn**

Looking for an external meaning to life can be a lot like analyzing a painting that appears to be nothing more than mud haphazardly tossed onto a canvas—at best, it's abstract and baffling, and somehow beautiful. Even without knowing what concrete unifying purpose our collective existence has, we can find peace and empowerment in a life focused on learning. It's a far more consistently visible purpose than any others we could adopt. Learning facilitates growth, which we can measure in an infinite number of ways over time.

You can't always do everything well in life, but you can get better from one day to the next. You can't ever know everything, but you can learn something new every day. In making the proactive choice to see every event as an opportunity to evolve—even the painful, disappointing, or disheartening experiences—you can nurture the powerful incentive to move forward, both in spite of and because of your struggles. You can look back at where you've been and how far you've come, and feel a sense of pride in the change you've created. And when you look around at the surroundings you've chosen, consciously or otherwise, you can know that if ever they become unsatisfying, you can transform them and yourself again and again. It's not only an available option—it's a deeply satisfying driving need. You can't ever control the world around you, but you can consistently choose how you adapt and transform within it.

Through learning, you can become anything;
through growth, you can make sense of
anything. *"*

What's particularly beautiful about learning is that it implies an ever-evolving internal, not just external, world. One day you might believe your purpose has everything to do with the passion that dominates your thoughts first thing in the morning, last thing at night, and every moment in between. The next day you might decide your new purpose requires you to create a sense of balance between doing and being. One day your life may seem to revolve around holding everyone around you together. The next day you might decide you need to learn to take care of your own needs, and that your purpose is to become adept at taking care of yourself. Implicit in learning and growing is the idea that we'll continually transform our understanding of our purpose and intentions. It's an abstract that propels you from one tangible to another—one goal, one passion, or one intention to the next. Learning is a lot like gravity: it's an invisible but powerful force that affects you whether you register it or not. You are always learning and growing. Through learning, you can become anything; through growth, you can make sense of anything.

Recently a woman named Jen Saunders contributed her first post to *TinyBuddha.com*. She and her boyfriend had moved to China to teach English to children. When they arrived, the principal informed them that he had accidentally hired them both for one job and then promptly fired Jen. She'd turned her life upside down to make this yearlong commitment, leaving her friends and family behind, and without any warning the dream imploded before she ever had a chance to explore it. To make matters worse, she got so sick that she had to spend a full month confined to her bed—in a foreign country, without her usual support system, and without a shred of purpose or sense of direction.

From the outside, you might gather that the world had fallen apart around her. It would have been easy for her to feel negative and victimized, wondering why her. Why did she get fired? Why did she have to get sick? Why did she have to face feelings of failure when she didn't do anything wrong? But Jen didn't go down that road. She decided instead that her sickness was teaching her something—that her emotions weren't in balance. And if she committed herself, she could learn to live an enriching life that inspired her even more than the one she thought she wanted would have. The simple act of deciding to learn from something that appeared senseless helped her make peace with it and sense of it. What could have been an anchor suddenly became a lighthouse, because she chose to learn and grow.

Meaningful transformation is a choice. *"*

Biology cites growth as one of the defining characteristics of life. Whether we realize it or not, we are always growing. We start as just one infinitesimal cell that divides into two and then into four until eventually we grow from infants to children to adults with upward of seventy-five trillion cells. Almost every cell in our body regenerates over a seven-year period, meaning that, in a very real way, we become a new person without ever choosing to. Our emotional lives parallel our biology in that way—it's inevitable that we'll grow in response to the world around us whether we choose change or not. Life hands us growth on a silver platter. Evolution defines our lives. Meaningful transformation, on the other hand, is a choice.

Pursue lifelong growth.

To create and measure growth for a sense of progress:

At the start of each day, ask yourself, "How can I apply today what I learned about myself yesterday?" Maybe you got in a fight with a friend and realized that you get defensive about certain hot-button topics. How can you learn from that to become more self-aware and relate better with friends today? Maybe you realized that you're not happy spending so much time on your computer. How can you make small adjustments in your schedule to disconnect from technology today?

Decide to do something every day that stretches yourself. Take a risk, small or large. Try something new, whether it's a food, a hobby, or a way of being. Get just a little outside your comfort zone to see how you can grow and flourish. There are limitless possibilities for you in life if you're willing to open your world a little every day.

Continues

Commit to comparing yourself only to former versions of you. Comparing yourself to other people is an exercise in self-torture because you can only be you, where you are, at any point in time. Instead, think about how far you've come from where you were. But the point isn't to become the best version of yourself, either—there is no end point you're aiming for. It's to continually grow, a little every day, and realize that the journey *is* the destination.

It is up to us to give life meaning

When we try giving labels to life, we lose the opportunity of being in the now. So forget the meaning; just experience it. ~**@soulsutras**

The meaning of life is to live life. Not just exist in it. ~**@Cadillac_Creek**

To give life meaning is to restrict the most beautiful to a mere idea. "Meaning" in life is found only through living now. ~**@MrWaffleable**

The meaning of life is to give meaning to your life. That your final thoughts be of a life well lived. A life well loved. ~**@Craig_Rattigan**

In itself, life is meaningless. It is we who attribute meaning to life. ~**@getkaizer**

I received hundreds of responses when I asked on Twitter, "What's the meaning of life?" The most common answer, which you don't see anywhere in this chapter—well, other than right here—was 42. If I had been familiar with *The Hitchhiker's Guide to the Galaxy,* I would have caught the reference and understood. Though I was clearly pop-culture deficient, I knew it must be from some movie or book. I also knew there were a lot of people who weren't inclined to offer a concrete answer and others who verbalized that very sentiment in their tweets. As Google's Chade-Meng tweeted in response to my question, "The meaning of life is not."

You could come at this quandary from multiple angles, looking for different scientific, religious, and philosophical perspectives as to why we're all here—or as Albert Camus pondered, why we shouldn't all kill ourselves. What exactly makes life valuable and worth living? What are we supposed to do? Where's it all leading? Is there someone or something guiding us to something better, something we can achieve if only we do something specific here and now? Jean-Paul Sartre wrote that "life has no meaning the moment you lose the illusion of being eternal." But does that mean we need to know where we came from or where we're going to choose to use this moment in a way that feels meaningful to us?

Is life so miserable that we need to understand the end to justify this experience as a means? It can be if we get so caught up in our desires and pains that life loses all its pleasure. Or if we convince ourselves there has to be something better than this, instead of using all our energy to make the best of this. Do we need to understand there's reward or punishment later in order to do good now? Sure, if doing good didn't have some value in itself, but it does. Doing good feels good, mentally, emotionally, and even physically—in that way giving is, in fact, its own reward.

There are a lot of things we may never understand, including whether or not what we do in this lifetime has any eternal, intrinsic value. Even if we did have answers instead of a million and one debatable questions, we'd probably still find reasons to argue, because we all have unique perspectives and could interpret those answers differently.

Maybe that's a beautiful thing. Infinite meanings to life equal each and every one of us fitting in this life. On any day, we can wake up and decide the type of person we want to be—whether we want to be brave, joyful, or daring—and then embody those qualities through our actions. On any day, we can decide to let go of our old stories and write new ones. On any day, we can decide to discard an old goal and create one that better aligns with what matters to us individually. We get to decide what it all means, just like we decide what the events themselves mean. When our world crumbles around us, leaving us desperately hopeful for an answer, we can decide it means it's over or that it's just beginning. When someone we love leaves our life, we can decide it means they took all hope of joy with them or that they left a space for something new that will fulfill us like we never knew to imagine. The meaning of every event starts and ends with our interpretations.

What's the meaning of life? I have no idea. Perhaps a better question is: "what are we doing about the things that are meaningful to us?"

CHANGE

CAN PEOPLE CHANGE,
AND HOW?

~~~~~~~~~~

"Some people never change."

That's the type of disheartening realization that we often form when someone's disappointed us. And it happens all through life. You put your faith in a person everyone else has given up on and, despite your idealism, he lets you down. You give someone a second chance, or a third, fourth, and hundredth, and even though it shouldn't surprise you, you feel a little dumbfounded when she takes advantage of your trust or kindness. Or maybe it was you who didn't change—who has tried again and again to scrub your spots away, only to succumb to the belief that perhaps they are permanent. Sometimes change can feel near impossible. But is it literally?

With the right amount of will and determination, can anyone change?

For a long time, the leading research suggested that our personalities were fixed in childhood, and from those personalities stemmed our behaviors. In 1884, the scientist Sir Francis Galton proposed the lexical hypothesis—the idea that we've created words for the most important and socially significant personality differences between us. In 1936, Gordon Allport and H. S. Odbert identified nearly eighteen thousand personality-describing words, which have been narrowed down through time and further investigation into the Big Five, as these are referred to: openness to experience, agreeableness, conscientiousness, neuroticism, and extroversion. These evolved from extensive research into personality and language.

We all possess all of these attributes to some degree, but we rank in different percentiles. No one is completely neurotic or, on the flip side, 100 percent emotionally stable. No one is a total extrovert or introvert. The newest research suggests that our personalities aren't ever set in stone, but rather evolve and mature over time. We are never stagnant, and if we allow ourselves, we can learn and grow all through our lives. While some employers still rely on personality testing to gauge our suitability for jobs, the good news is that we don't ever have to pigeonhole ourselves into specific, defined ways of being. We don't have to believe that we are powerless to change things about our personalities. It might be uncomfortable to learn new tricks, but it *is* possible. Whether or not we actually learn them is largely dependent on what we believe.

For a long time I lived with two conflicting beliefs that, had I kept them, would have ensured I could never change what I did, how I felt, or how I experienced the world. I can trace their roots back to when I started running, in late 2001, after I had decided the only way to eclipse my emotional pain was to physically escape it.

Before my time in NYC, I moved from Massachusetts to Washington State to live with a stranger I met on the Internet. I figured the best way to overcome my misery was to get far away fast from the scene of my adolescent crimes—my self-imposed isolation and everything I did to numb myself. Six months later, I crossed the country on an Amtrak train, disappointed that a relationship built on a foundation about as strong as a house of cards hadn't saved me from myself.

It wasn't until after I'd toured the United States for six months with marketing companies that I decided to transplant myself to the city where dreams come true. I believed my greatest strength was my courage—that I was willing to take massive risks and change homes and jobs in a heartbeat. What underlay that need for change was a far less romantic belief: that my only hope of happiness was to somehow out-run myself. I would never have guessed that constant movement can be paralyzing, but that's exactly what I learned in New York City.

It wasn't until I was curled up in the fetal position in my fifth-floor filth, shortly after my aspiring entrepreneur "friends" Rich and Jim left, that I began considering that my misfortune might be a gift. Later, as I sat at my window chain-smoking, swigging whiskey, and staring down at the throng of other suburban transplants I was afraid might not like me, I realized no one could possibly like me less than I liked myself. I was in the perfect position to implement change.

I had no one to distract me from the root of my disillu-sionment with myself. No one was going to hand me a per-mission slip to wait it out. No one was about to cast me to live permanently in someone else's vision. It didn't matter where I lived; it would always be a prison if I didn't learn to be part of the world. It didn't matter how much money I made; it would just buy me more pairs of high heels that looked ridic-ulous under my underachieving, bug-infested bed. It didn't matter if I had a job I loved; it would just be a bigger distrac-tion from the truth that I didn't love myself. Right then, in a completely imperfect world, the time was perfect to work on myself. I had only one choice: choose something to do with my life and muster the courage to start.

A week later, I signed up to volunteer at a yoga studio in exchange for free classes. I'd taken a few classes before, and I remembered experiencing two powerful things: a deep sense of inner calm as my slowed breathing decelerated my thoughts and agonizing discomfort as the teacher pushed my legs deeper into a hip-opening pose. I wanted more of both the peace and the pain—the former, because it felt good, and the latter because I wanted to do better at getting through the inevitable moments when life wouldn't.

Every night at 6:00, without fail, I grabbed my yoga mat from under my raised twin-size bed and walked the three streets to the studio. No matter how I felt during the day, no matter what I had accomplished, or hadn't, I made my way back to my mat.

During my time staffing the front of the studio, I got the opportunity to learn a lot about the owner. She told me she'd smoked for almost a decade and was slowly healing herself. I wasn't quite there yet. More times than I care to admit, I stood on the corner of Thirty-seventh and Eighth clutching my yoga mat in one hand and a cigarette in the other, imagining the wafting smoke branded me the world's biggest hypocrite. I couldn't just be proud of taking a positive step; I had to berate myself for not leaping over the massive chasm between who I was and who I wanted to be.

At the end of every yoga class, everyone does one final pose known as *savasana*. It's when you let your body absorb the effects of the class by lying in stillness for a few moments on your mat. Something about being all sweaty and exposed, closing my eyes, and relaxing in a room of other people made me feel a little like vomiting. At the end of most classes, I tiptoed out of the room while other students were melting into a blissful state of openness and peace. But one night, about two months in, I challenged myself to stay. At first my body opposed this plan. My arms and legs jittered and my teeth chattered while I felt an overall magnetic pull toward the door. Even after a class of moving meditation, I wanted to get back to my cave. I told myself that I could fight it all I wanted but I wouldn't be getting up for three minutes and that, if I chose to, I might even enjoy it. Miraculously, it worked. I don't know that I'd ever experienced a state of calm being with so little resistance, at least not while left alone inside my own head.

After class, I felt completely unburdened by my usual angst, fear, and containment. I even complimented one woman on her multicolored yoga bag. I told another woman her practice inspired me. And then I said yes when she asked me to grab a bite to eat.

I instantly regretted it. She might not be as friendly outside the studio. I might want to leave but feel trapped in conversation with her. And worst of all, I wouldn't be able to smoke for at least another hour. As we walked to the sandwich place down the street, I fidgeted with my hair and bit my nails, trying to satisfy the nervous energy that was screaming at me to run home and stuff five Marlboros into my mouth to make up for lost time.

I would like to say I remember even one single thing she said, but to this day I have no idea. All I know is that she *did* speak words, and physically I was capable of hearing and understanding them, but my thoughts were way too loud to allow it. All the openness I had created in class filled up with a swarm of anxieties and fears, but I'd passed the point of no return; the only option was to get through this meal. I'd push through it, like I pushed through so many other uncomfortable moments, and then run back to safety as soon as I could. It could be like it never happened. I'd be alone soon enough.

At some point during my inner diatribe, my cigarette pack fell out of my pocket. Maybe I was willing it out with my mind. Or maybe it wasn't my friend after all. Maybe my habit was trying to sabotage this new relationship, which would clearly have been deep and fulfilling had I not just proven myself a poser—and not the yoga kind. Whatever the case, I was outed. I was not what I seemed. I was a fraud. I hadn't changed at all. I was weak and intrinsically bad.

I take back what I wrote earlier. I will never forget one thing my classmate said when she saw the pack and then heard my confession of meaning to quit: "Good for you, honey. It can be so hard. Keep coming back to class. You'll get there."

This woman who hardly knew me, whom I'd been secretly plotting to desert, was unconditionally compassionate and kind to me. She didn't focus on what I was doing wrong; she didn't hone in on my inability to instantaneously transform my life into the picture of health and happiness. She didn't judge me for being flawed or form general assumptions about who I was based on my challenges. Instead, she recognized that I'd made a positive choice and that, if I kept at it, I could change over time. She saw me as a complete package—the sum of my strengths and my weaknesses. I was not someone to be ashamed of; I was someone to be proud of. There was nothing wrong with me. My choices could use improvement, and I was working on that. I was not a weak person; I just gave in to weakness sometimes. I was not a bad person; I just made bad choices sometimes. Regardless of all of that, I deserved understanding. I was not someone to escape; I was someone to love.

The very act of making a different choice is in itself change. *"*

We are all people worth loving, regardless of what behaviors we may want to change—and we all have the power to change, even if on some days our resistance feels about as overpowering as a riptide. We may not always open ourselves up to new possibilities, but that doesn't mean we're unable. We may have days when we're not very friendly or compassionate, but that doesn't mean we have to experience every day guarded and closed off. We might experience high levels of stress and insecurity, but that doesn't imply we'll always experience the world with a sense of worry and fear. On any given day, we can change the way we act and interact with other people. The very act of making a different choice is in itself change. Whether or not we can sustain those changes depends largely on what we believe and what we tell ourselves.

Most people are far more compassionate and patient with other people than they are with themselves. You'd probably never tell your friend that she's worthless if she was having trouble changing her eating habits. You likely wouldn't berate your mother for feeling too scared to go out and meet new people. And yet you form overarching conclusions about yourself and your character based on your own shortcomings and setbacks. We expect immediate results and get frustrated and disappointed when we don't feel like we're making progress fast enough. If change isn't instantaneous—if we can't recognize it through consider-able alterations to the world as we know it—we assume it isn't happening. That feeling of resignation is precisely what keeps us stuck or, perhaps more accurately, feeling stuck.

We can get unstuck at any time—that much is clear. What can be slightly more confusing is *how*. With that in mind, I asked on Twitter, "Can people change, and how?"

Change starts in our mind

People can change when they realize that the pleasure of changing is greater than the pain of staying the same. ~**@AdamHansen**

One of the reasons people change is because they educate themselves. ~**@Queen_Isis_24**

People can and will change by realizing the difference between what they think and who they are and acting on it. ~**@MrWaffleable**

Change happens when we stop identifying with our ideas, opinions, concepts, beliefs, and judgments. ~**@mullet3000**

People change as soon as they try to see themselves from a different angle. ~**@skaterearth**

Since the advent of the personal-development industry, we've become increasingly determined to improve ourselves. In 2007, the *National Post* (Canada) referred to professional coaching as the second-fastest-growing career in the United States. Though this form of coaching is primarily geared toward achieving professional success, it involves identifying and challenging fears, attitudes, and thoughts that inhibit growth. We all have them, and sometimes we're so determined to see outward change that we skip the vital step of evaluating the beliefs that stand in the way.

Henry Ford said, "Whether you think you can or you can't, you're right." The same is true for change: if you don't believe you can, you can't. We form beliefs all throughout our lives that limit the choices we make. Sometimes that's a good thing. If you believe you are a kind person and that kind people look out for others, that will limit your choices, too, but insomuch as it prevents you from kicking someone else in the face or stealing her thunder at work. In that regard, the belief guides you to choices that make you feel good about yourself.

But that's not how beliefs always work. Sometimes our beliefs directly oppose our wants and leave us feeling stuck and bewildered. What makes it all the more perplexing is that we often confuse facts and beliefs. Facts are nonnegotiable; beliefs are interpretations. We don't always recognize the difference.

When I started my first blog, prior to *TinyBuddha.com*, I wrote a post called "10 Reasons It's Awesome the Economy Sucks." I had a feeling it would elicit a strong response because most people react to decreased financial security with terror and stress. My theory was that we can feel an increased sense of personal power if we change what we believe about the immutable facts of the economic meltdown.

Fact: Unemployment requires lifestyle changes. When you make that first uncomfortable sacrifice, you may decide that you can't possibly be happy in your new reality because it will continue to be challenging. Once you do that, you'll likely look for evidence to back it up. Every time you have to go without something, you'll make a mental note of how much better things were before, and how right you were to resist this new reality. The alternative is to challenge that belief when you're inclined to form it. Instead of assuming all sacrifices will be painful, you can decide it will give you an opportunity to be resourceful and channel gratitude for what you still have. The belief you form will dictate how you feel, what you think, and how you act. The limiting belief keeps you unhappy and closed off; the other one opens you up to possibilities.

Psychologists suggest that we don't hold on to a belief unless there's some type of payoff in doing it. We wouldn't willfully choose to feel trapped and unhappy. We hold on to these beliefs because they give us something we think we need. So let's say that you want to improve your financial situation, but when you were growing up, your parents always referred to wealthy people with choice expletives. You may have formed the belief that you can't possibly be both a good person and well-off. No matter how hard you work to improve your situation, you'll feel an intrinsic pull toward self-sabotage. The payoff? You don't have to deal with the discomfort of thinking that you're somehow a bad person.

The hard thing about beliefs is that sometimes they serve a temporary purpose but later become unnecessary. At twelve years old, I formed a belief that if I didn't leave my house, I was less likely to hurt. At the time, it was true. Since I was tormented in school, it made sense that if I didn't show up, kids couldn't hurt me. Granted, that wasn't the only way to escape the pain of their harassment—and clearly was not a proactive approach to changing things—but it was certainly one way to avoid those uncomfortable feelings. It was a valid belief: stay away from the cause and I minimize the effect. Later in time, it no longer served me. Staying inside caused me lots of pain because we social creatures weren't made to be contained.

The other day I read an article on *PsychologyToday. com* that cited a fascinating study about limiting beliefs. Researchers put a glass wall in the middle of a long aquarium.

Every time the goldfish inside tried to cross the tank, they banged their little scaly heads into the wall. Over time, they became conditioned to stick to one side to avoid the pain they'd come to expect. Even after the researchers eventually removed the glass partition, the fish never tried to explore the other side. Their limiting belief kept them confined to the world they had always known—even though they clearly wanted to know the other side at one point in time, and they could easily access it now.

We carry around so many different beliefs that we often don't even recognize some of them. We just know what feels good, what feels bad, and which one of the two we prefer. The thing is, we don't always realize how good things can feel on the other side of how they are. We don't recognize that being healthy might feel better than comfort eating, or that trying something new might be infinitely more satisfying than staying with the familiar. We don't always realize how close we are to knowing a new world that's even more fulfilling than we ever knew to imagine.

Can changing your mind change your life? Not in and of itself, but you have to change your mind to change your choices, and that will affect your life.

Challenge limiting beliefs to create change.

If you suspect that your beliefs are holding you back:

Make a list of your "I can't change" excuses. Start with the simple question: *Why can't I (lose weight, quit smoking, maintain a healthy relationship, change jobs, etc.).* Now write down everything that comes to mind—all the different things you believe to be true. Do you think you can't lose weight because you're too weak? Or you can't quit smoking because your job is stressful? Or you can't have a healthy relationship because you have too much baggage?

Highlight everything that's not a proven fact. Go through your excuses with the intent to poke holes in them. Some of them may be valid, but many will be limiting beliefs disguised as facts. It's not a proven fact that you're weak. It's not a proven fact that someone with a stressful job needs to smoke to deal with it. It's not a proven fact that you have "too much baggage" (how much is the right amount exactly?) or that people with baggage can't be happy in relationships. (I'm living proof!) It may help to imagine that your best friend is feeding you these excuses about his own life. What beliefs would you challenge in him?

"Why?" your way to freedom. Ask yourself: *Why* do I believe this—when did I form this belief? Did it come from someone else or my environment? *Why* am I holding on to it—what's the payoff for me? Does it allow me to feel better about not taking action? Does it feel safe? *Why* is it so important that I let this go—what amazing conditions could I create if I considered the possibility this belief isn't fact? *Why* am I talking to myself instead of doing something today to change this situation I so clearly want to change?

You have to really want to change

People can change, but they have to want to. It requires courage and the willingness to experience all that comes with change. ~@**quietdream625**

People change when they can stop lying to themselves. The truth will set you free. ~@**miss_morrison**

The desire to change from within is crucial to progress forward on a different path. ~@**FeliciaOnFire**

Growth allows for change. As long as people continue to grow, spiritually and mentally, change is indeed possible. ~@**HauteinLA**

In order to be somewhere new, you have to know where you are and why you want to go. ~@**MsEmilyAnarchy**

Something very interesting happens in our brains when we experience change in our environment. Remember that fight-or-flight response I mentioned before, along with the amygdala? That same fear conditioning pushes us into panic mode when something in our environment changes. Interestingly, Buddhist monks who engage in compassion meditation are believed to regulate their amygdala; by tempering their fear response and other emotional defenses, they're best able to open their hearts. If we want to open ourselves up to change, we essentially need to do the same thing.

Have you ever felt certain that you wanted to make a positive change in your life, only to find yourself coming up against massive internal resistance? You knew the benefits and you had the best intentions, but subconsciously, you were trudging through quicksand. It's not that there's something wrong with you for struggling to muster motivation or push through discomfort. Your brain is creating a roadblock to what you think you want—it's pushing you to question whether you even want it at all, considering how scary and different it is. It's precisely why we say we want one thing and then do the exact opposite—why I spent years saying I wanted to be part of the world but then nearly hyperventilated whenever I spent too much time in an uncontrollable environment. The amygdala senses colossal change and then braces us for impending doom.

Jeffrey Schwartz, author of *The Mind and the Brain*, explains how our brains form ideas that limit our ability to change. The things we repeatedly tell ourselves create "mental maps" that prepare us for what to expect in life. Then we tend to experience reality exactly as we anticipated it, whether it's actually that way or not.

A good friend of mine is always telling me she doesn't enjoy her work and she'd like to do something more fulfilling and lucrative with her time. Yet she never researches other careers, looks into taking classes, or even tries to visualize a future that involves a job that isn't mind-numbingly boring to her. She devotes a significant amount of her energy to lamenting the way things aren't without ever doing anything to change how they are. I suspect it has a lot to do with two critical pieces of her past: she has an advanced degree that has not yet helped her land a great job, and she's been fired from several jobs she didn't love. Based on our conversations, I've surmised that she believes no matter what she does, she can't get a good job—and even if she does, she'll probably somehow mess it up. If she's using the mental map she built based on past experiences, that logic might make sense. But the future doesn't have to repeat itself. She has a choice in how it unfolds.

The best way to navigate new territory is to create new mental maps. Research indicates that we do this most effectively when we reach our own insights, as opposed to when someone else tells us what to do. It's why advice so frequently falls flat: in order for us to get past the discomfort of our thoughts and conditioning, we truly need to have our own epiphanies. It doesn't matter if I tell my friend a million times she could change her life by switching careers. She has to reach that conclusion on her own.

So how do we reach these new conclusions? How can we even begin to implement change when we're not fully on board, and nothing anyone else tells us can change that? How can we challenge our own resistance when our resistance is just as strong as, if not stronger than, our desire? Awareness is the first step. They say to name a thing is to have power over it. Once we realize that there is something biological at play, it's a lot easier to step outside ourselves and plan to circumnavigate it. So it isn't that we're weak or incapable; it's that we need a little more material to build an effective new mental map.

We do that by gathering one little piece at a time. Oftentimes we think if we're not affecting major change, then change isn't happening—but all that does is cause us anxiety, triggering that good old amygdala. Massive change will always be scary, but small, manageable steps slowly reprogram your expectations for the life you're creating. If you brainstorm about possible jobs and then make two calls today, you'll see that taking one simple proactive step isn't nearly as terrifying at it seems. Once you get that down, you might consider calling a few more. Once again, there's no reason to anticipate disaster. The same can be said for starting a new exercise program. If you're usually inactive and you try to run a marathon, you'll likely be overwhelmed and disappointed in yourself. Jogging for ten minutes, on the other hand, sets you up for a greater chance of success.

Every now and then, I ask on Twitter, "Is there anything I can do to help or support you today?" It's my way of reminding whoever might be reading that we are not alone, and someone somewhere is there to help. Recently someone asked me, "What do you do when you feel like your whole world is crashing down on you?" I responded, "I stop trying to put it all back together for a bit and let myself deal with my feelings. Then I start rebuilding one piece at a time."

It's the only way anything can change—one small piece at a time. Not only is it compassionate to let yourself operate without the pressure to instantaneously transform, it's also the smartest way to deal with the mental challenges you, and every single one of us, face.

Create a new mental map.

To start creating incremental change:

Identify the pain this way of being causes you. Psychologist Edgar Schein has identified three precursors to a change in behavior: a sense that the situation causes pain or dissatisfaction; survival anxiety, which is the awareness that you will be more uncomfortable if you don't change; and psychological safety, which means that you feel safe to explore and make mistakes without fear of repercussions. Start with the pain: What pain is this behavior causing you? Are you struggling financially because of it? Is it putting your health at risk and limiting your day-to-day joy?

Continues

Enlist help to form your own insights. This also falls under the umbrella of "psychological safety." It always feels a lot easier to explore new possibilities when you have the support of a friend, coach, therapist, or group. The goal here is to challenge the expectations and attitudes that are keeping you conflicted and stuck. Don't run to the friend who is always doling out advice like everyone's personal guru. You need someone who is going to help you unlearn and relearn for yourself. The goal is to have your own epiphany about the attitudes that are keeping you paralyzed.

Make one small behavioral change at a time. Once you feel certain, for yourself, that you truly want to make this change, start with one behavior at a time. Don't try to change everything you don't like about your life at once. Instead, choose one behavior, knowing you may not always do it perfectly, and work to make it a routine. It will help if you create some type of system for positive feedback, whether that means charting your own successes or joining a support group. When you feel good about what you're doing, it naturally requires less effort.

Consistency creates change

People can change, but consistency is key. With consistency and stability, clarity and maturity soon follow. ~**@YogaStudioSouth**

Change requires open-heart[ed] reflecting on what one really wants to change, catching that behavior and modifying it, little at a time. ~**@glaughlin**

By remembering to act and think like the person you want to be, it gradually becomes who you are. ~**@debismyname**

People change only if they really want to and they work on it every day. ~@ngageguy

People change by conscious living and awareness. ~@amourabunny

Sometimes we have the best intentions of being consistent, but life gets in the way. Case in point: Once upon a time, I'd set my alarm clock to 5:30 AM if that was my only option for exercising. This past year, the only body parts I moved with consistency were my wrists and my mouth. Every night before I went to sleep, I told Ehren, my boyfriend, that exercise makes me energized, centered, and happy when I take the time to do it regularly. Despite knowing the benefits, and how I'd feel once I made exercise a routine again, I kept a well-worn list of excuses to de-prioritize fitness. It usually revolved around my busy schedule, but I suspect there were two bigger reasons. First, I was embracing an all-or-nothing attitude. If I couldn't exercise for two hours a day, like I used to years ago, I didn't want to do it at all. And second, since I'm actually quite petite, albeit kind of mushy, I wasn't uncomfortable enough to push myself through change. Still, the point remains, it was something I said I wanted, but then I often failed to do it.

Most of us can relate to wanting to change something but then losing steam before seeing any results. You'll find tens of thousands of articles online about how to form a new habit, most suggesting it takes twenty-one days to ingrain a new routine so that it becomes instinctive, as opposed to requiring steel-strong will. However, research reveals that this isn't actually a hard-and-fast scientific fact. Maxwell Maltz originated this idea in his book *Psycho-Cybernetics: A New Way to Get More Living Out of Life*. Maltz explained that amputees generally experience phantom sensations where their limbs previously were for twenty-one days after the loss. From there, Maltz theorized our brains only produce neural pathways and connections if we do something for twenty-one days in a row. After that period, any new behavior becomes a rote way of living.

> **P**erhaps the best question isn't how long does it take to maintain a life change, but rather, how can we deal with the emotions that get in the way of forming a new routine? //

Later research has suggested there is no magic number—no universal sweet spot for adopting a behavior that suddenly becomes automatic and easy to maintain. There also isn't any concrete proof that we need to pile up a certain number of back-to-back days or all of our efforts are for naught. It may be helpful to create that type of regularity since we're less likely to revert to old behaviors if we believe every day is important, but on the flip side, this just exacerbates that black-and-white thinking that suggests it's all or nothing. It isn't.

Perhaps the best question isn't how long does it take to maintain a life change, but rather, how can we deal with the emotions that get in the way of forming a new routine? Even if we know intellectually things may be better if we change, how do we get ourselves to remember it will not only be better but also absolutely worth it to push through the discomfort of change? How do we motivate ourselves in that moment when we're feeling all kinds of challenging things that compel us to give up?

It isn't easy to sit with our emotions, and sometimes they occur so quickly after stimulus that we fail to recognize they are two separate events: what happens and how we feel about it. In response to those feelings, we crave things: a cigarette, a drink, a doughnut, or even just the consistency of the way things already are—when you don't have to do anything other than what you know feels good. Ultimately, it all comes back to pain and pleasure: we're wired to do what's enjoyable and resist what isn't, and sometimes short-term pleasure trumps the long-term happiness we intellectually know a change will create.

The best thing we can do when we're feeling things that make it tempting to stay the same is to create space between the feeling and the behavior—to recognize that the two don't need to go together. If you usually eat your feelings, but just once during the day you sit with your discomfort for five or ten minutes before opening the fridge, the next day you can build on that and slowly recondition the way you experience and deal with emotions. It's not immediate change—and this might not be the first day of a lifetime abiding by a new habit. But what's important is us starting the change from within by pushing ourselves to challenge what we think we want and need.

The best thing we can do when we're feeling things that make it tempting to stay the same is to create space between the feeling and the behavior.

In dealing with my resistance to exercise, I've recently been forcing myself to do nothing for ten minutes after I decide I'm not going to exercise. So instead of making the decision on impulse, because I'd rather watch a movie and then forgetting about the fact that exercise is something I actually want, I give myself space to recall why I want this. During this time, I inevitably remember how strong and healthy I used to feel. I remember how much I love physical activities that require endurance and how much progress I've been making. And I often realize that exercise isn't something bad that I'm forcing myself to do—it's something I want to do and enjoy. That's where consistency comes from: knowing what you want in the long term, understanding you may have conflicting wants in the short term, and creating sufficient space to decide what you're going to do about it.

Create consistency with a new behavior.

If you're struggling with creating a new habit:

Plan in advance. You are far more likely to exercise, eat healthy, or try something new if you write it down and plan for it. Schedule it to set yourself up for success—meaning, don't tell yourself that you'll exercise at 5:00 a.m. if you know you're not likely to do it, or plan to make phone calls on Saturday afternoon if you know you enjoy hiking then. Try to place the activity where you suspect you'll have minimal excuses not to do it.

If the thing you're trying to change is more mental—such as being defensive or dramatic—plan for triggers and new ways to address them. If you get defensive when people challenge your work, plan for how you will view things from a different angle. Maybe you'll consider the validity of what they're saying, or simply thank them for sharing how they see things and then work through it in your head later.

Create an accountability system. None of us has a steel-strong will, and sometimes when we're fighting with ourselves, the path of least resistance wins. Get other people on board with your plan. Blog or tweet about the

Continues

change you're trying to make. Tell a friend or family member. And then ask them to keep you accountable. Ask them to ask you every evening how it went—or even better, work with someone else who wants to make the same change with you.

Prepare for challenges. It's inevitable you will feel resistant at times, and you will have setbacks. Know in advance what you will do when this happens. It might mean sitting with your feelings, or calling a friend for motivation and support.

Focus on progress, not perfection. Say good-bye to black-and-white thinking. It's not about making complete and major changes right now. It's about making changes that bring you closer to where you want to be. Don't berate yourself for not exercising every day this week—that will just make you feel guilty and defeated. Instead, celebrate that you exercised twice, reward those successes, and then make a commitment to do more next week.

Our environment and the people around us affect our ability to sustain change

People can change but they tend to change back if their friends, family, and community fail to acknowledge it and treat them differently. ~@**MegEtc**

People can change with the help of others via compassion. Some people just need to be heard and supported. ~@**Flosara**

Human nature can't be changed. But a child can be raised and brought up to be a loving person, and that's a good start. ~@**AgaNY**

People can change if they want to and they have the tools either developed internally or by the help of others. ~@caltex

People change 'cause of their surroundings. ~ @Carolinelfje

Every now and then I like to people watch—to be somewhere with no objective other than to notice how everyone acts and interacts within that environment.

A few years back, I was sitting in the mall watching people in CVS. I saw an angry teenager and a mother with her toddler son on opposite sides of the same aisle. The teen was trying to steal something, and the mother was looking at cosmetics while her son picked up anything and everything that wasn't bolted down. Within a matter of seconds, the teenager got caught and the toddler knocked a bottle off the shelf, though luckily, it didn't break. While all the attention was on the shoplifter who was being brought to the back, the mother grabbed her two-year-old and hit him so hard across the face that I actually started shaking. I felt flushed and nauseated as two things occurred to me: If she'd been paying attention, he wouldn't have touched things, as kids tend to do. But far more disturbing, if she was willing to do that in public, what kind of cruelty did he endure at home?

As I ran to the security guard to report the abuse—while she called him stupid and dragged him out of the store—I remember thinking two more things. One: That boy could very well grow up to be the other kid in the store. And two: I wished I could pull him aside, endow him with adult-like comprehension, and then tell him that for the next eighteen years, he shouldn't believe a single thing his mother says. No matter how many insults she hurls his way, no matter how she undermines his character or potential, he isn't stupid and he is worthy of a far greater love. But naturally I couldn't do that. And even if I could protect him from the strongest influence in his life, I couldn't change everything else about his upbringing or environment. I couldn't change that he will be affected by the world around him, just as I was and am and just as you are.

Let's face it: we don't live in a vacuum. Our environment growing up shaped who we are, and our current environment influences who we are and who we become. You can put all your energy into being a more peaceful person, but if your roommate or spouse has a penchant for drama, you'll have your work cut out for you. You could spend countless hours channeling your inner Dalai Lama to combat stress, but if your work brings you face-to-face with violent criminals, you may find it challenging to let go of anxiety. That's not to say you have to give up on people or your job to feel how you want to feel. After all, we can always choose our attitude, regardless of our circumstances. But the conditions around us *do* affect us. Studies show that police officers have a life expectancy that's seven to twenty years lower than the average person, because of the stress that comes with the job. So while we may learn to cope well when faced with external challenges, they still take their toll, both emotionally and physically.

Luckily, most of us don't have to stay in environments that challenge how or who we want to be. Unlike when we were children, we as adults have a choice over our surroundings. We're never trapped in a home, job, relationship, friendship, or way of life that isn't working. We are never stuck. Much like we can choose what we do from day to day to create change, we can choose whether or not our environment facilitates or hinders those choices. Just like you might feng shui your home to align your atmosphere with your intentions, sometimes you need to feng shui your life—to cherry-pick the people, things, circumstances, and ideas that you allow to surround you. It all influences what you choose to do.

> **W**e can always choose our attitude, regardless of our circumstances. "

As with most things in life, it's a lot easier to talk about this theoretically than it is to actually make a major change in our life—or even to acknowledge we need to. One of the most difficult things to do is accept when something familiar is working against us and then change it for the better, particularly if it isn't a simple onetime decision. When I lived in that seedy dorm-style building, where a neighbor's overdose was a common occurrence, smoking cigarettes seemed like the least of all evils. In fact, a lot of demeaning choices felt natural when I viewed myself, my life, and my situation as hopeless and shameful. It took me a year to move out of that building, including the time it took to decide I could secure better-paying work and locate an affordable alternative. But until I accepted that I deserved something better, all my choices came from the belief that I didn't—including when I dated a Wall Street stockbroker who told me I was lucky he spent time with me since I wasn't really a good catch. I only became strong within that environment when I realized I could work to change it. Even if it didn't change overnight, the decision to work toward something better gave me the strength to make better choices in my everyday life.

> **E**verything that goes on around us affects what goes on within us. *"*

We all deserve the best in life, but only we can give it to ourselves. Only we can create the visions and manifest them. Only we can set boundaries and honor them. Only we can decide how we want to be treated and then move on from relationships when they don't reflect that. And only we can decide enough is enough when the world around us is more harmful than helpful.

The good news is that some of our environmental factors are much easier to change than others. It isn't just the big things that affect our behavior—the little things all add up, too. For example, if you put your sneakers next to the front door, this simple visual cue might help you be consistent with exercise. If you choose not to receive daily news updates or read emails from your negative cousin, it might be a lot easier to maintain a positive mind-set. And if you de-clutter and organize your personal space, getting organized professionally will most likely be a lot simpler.

Everything that goes on around us affects what goes on within us. Our thoughts, our feelings, our actions, our environment—they are all intertwined. Whenever we make a change in one, there's a ripple effect in the others. The question is: how do you want to experience change—in reaction to everything that happens to you, or as a proactive choice that dictates what will?

Create an optimal environment for change.

To ensure your surroundings set you up for success:

Assess the big picture environment: is anything working against you? Are you living with people who make you feel bad about yourself and, therefore, stuck? Is your neighborhood unsafe in a way that makes you feel limited in what you want to do? Does your work culture make it difficult to make the professional changes you want to make? Changing these things obviously won't be easy, but recognizing them is a vital first step. Where there is a will, there is a way. So ask yourself: is there a will?

Make changing that environment a priority. You can easily find a million and one excuses not to change the big things in life. But all the little things that this big thing limits are far more important than you realize. This one change could open the door to happiness like you've never experienced before. Make it your top priority. Once you're in a more positive living or work situation, or once you change the people you surround yourself with, it will be far easier to be the person you want to be.

Create environmental cues to help you make change. If you're trying to eat healthy, stock your refrigerator with the fruits and vegetables you most enjoy. If you're pushing yourself to pursue your dream, create a vision board and hang it somewhere you'll see it often. If you want to start meditating more often, get a really comfortable mat and make a meditation corner. Create space to be who you want to be, and you're more likely to occupy that space as that person.

Change is inevitable with everything in life

People and life change all the time. Saying yes to that is one of the paths that lead to change for the better. ~@moritherapy

Everything that is alive changes. We only stop changing when we cease to exist. ~@cattigan

Our lives are in constant motion and we as individuals are in a perpetual state of change, whether we realize it or not. ~@goodmangoes

Of course people can change. It's the only thing that we all do. ~@waltman

Change: lift your foot and stomp the earth. ~@kmaezenmiller

If there's one thing that's constant in life, it's change. Though we don't always realize it when we get comfortable or confident with the way things are, everything is always in flux. Just like we don't feel the earth rotating or realize how much time is going by, change doesn't depend on our registering it. It happens every hour, every minute, and every second of every day. So much can change in a heartbeat, and so much often does without our even noticing.

We can't change that life always changes, but we can learn to change with it. *"*

Every day the people around us change. They develop new skills, form new relationships, learn new lessons, and essentially become new people. Every day the children around us change—sometimes so quickly we forget to enjoy them until just before they crawl, walk, talk, or leave the house with a little less innocence. Every day our relationships change. One day, intimacy makes you feel like part of another person; tomorrow the distance can feel palpable, like an earthquake split the ground between you. The next day, you feel familiarly close again, but it won't be the same as it used to be, as it never was anything permanent. Nothing ever is.

Every day your business changes. In fact, a competitive company is always transforming, innovating, rolling out new products, and developing strategies to stay relevant. Your job might seem consistent and secure, but you never know when your role may develop into something different or even become obsolete. You never know when you might want it to change—when all of a sudden yesterday's predictabilities will seem more tedious than safe.

Every day our environment changes. Even if you never leave your hometown, the world you know and trust will slowly change shape and flavor. One day a strip mall will stand where your childhood playground was, or a construction company will start development on a chain restaurant where your favorite mom-and-pop shop used to be. Other businesses will come and go. Buildings will get demolished and new ones erected in their place. Roads will get resurfaced. Old neighbors will move out while new ones come in. Demographics will change, new politicians will take office, and your urban area will be gentrified, or your suburban area urbanized.

Everything changes. The weather changes. The seasons change. The economy changes. Times change. Health changes. People change. Nothing ever stays the same—and that can be scary if you sit in one place and identify every little nuance of difference, considering life a time-lapse video you wish you could pause. Or it can be endlessly fulfilling if you consider that every moment is a new opportunity to be the person you want to be. It is. As soon as you decide to let go of the way things were, you're able to find possibilities in the way things are.

We can't change that life always changes, but we can learn to change with it. We can stop interpreting every ending as a death and instead look for the rebirth in new beginnings. Does that mean we can dramatically alter our personality? That we can change who we are at our core, defy other people's expectations, and become better than our weaknesses? Maybe the more important questions are: Does any of that even matter? Why should we have to fight with who we are when we always have the means to change what we do?

Can people change? Absolutely. It's the only thing everyone and everything does. We just have to choose—in one moment, and then in the next.

FATE

DOES EVERYTHING HAPPEN
FOR A REASON?

It's comforting to believe that everything happens for a reason—that there's some universal plan guiding us toward exactly what we need, either for this life or the next one. When you believe in this type of fate, everything feels purposeful and even, if not controllable, understandable. If you get sick, you could say God has given you the illness to strengthen your spirit. If you get in a car accident, you could say the Universe is teaching you to slow down and enjoy the journey more. Or broadly speaking, if you come up against any type of overwhelming adversity, you can take solace in the fact that nothing happens unless it's precisely what you need. That's Mira Kirshenbaum's theory, anyway. Her book

Everything Happens for a Reason is a detailed guide to the value inherent in every difficulty.

She offers precisely ten reasons that something might happen in life, and they are all both useful and reassuring. Whether it's to help us accept ourselves, feel forgiveness, become stronger, find love, or live with purpose, in Kirshenbaum's world, everything is all about us—and all in our favor. I understand the allure of finding meaning in things that happen, and believing something bigger than ourselves is supporting us, weaving events together for our ultimate benefit and growth. The alternative is to accept that everything is random—that cause and effect exist, that what we do influences what we experience, but still the world at large is chaotic and unpredictable.

You might assume the latter is the less spiritual or empowering interpretation, but is it really? If we choose to learn and grow from the things that happen to us, is it even necessary to guess at why they happened? What's a more productive use of our energy—searching for meaning outside ourselves or creating meaning within ourselves?

I have always had a fascination with permanent disfigurement. It's an odd and somewhat embarrassing confession, I know. I've read a ton about victims of war, fire, abuse, and animal attacks because I am in awe of the strength it takes to go on after such devastating trauma. How does someone even begin to rebuild himself when he can no longer recognize the face he sees in the mirror? How does someone learn to move on when she has a visual reminder of the most painful and terrifying moment of her life? In a society where people often judge before offering compassion, how does a scarred cover find the will to contain a positive book? The closest I've ever come to an answer was in the middle of Ohio. To explain how I found myself there, I have to return once again to New York.

In 2006, I was ready to leave the city for good. I'd been practicing yoga for over a year, I'd quit smoking, and I had started looking a lot less like a malnourished, stress-case mess on legs. Having moved into a cockroach-free efficiency studio and saved up some cash through contract marketing work, I felt confident I had learned what I was meant to learn—how to take care of myself and bounce back from adversity instead of dwelling in self-pity. I was far from perfect, but I was beginning to care less about that, and that felt like a major success. Couple that with my renewed sense of health and rejuvenation, and I was ready to conquer the world.

My journey away from the Big Apple involved six million steps west. I saw an ad online for a fitness-related marketing tour called Steps Across America. Sportline, a company that makes pedometers, was sponsoring this promotional effort to increase awareness about the benefits of walking. They were looking for twelve people to form a relay team that would cross the United States on foot over three months—while blogging about it.

The opportunity seemed to be made for me. I'd been working so hard to improve my health, starting with my attitude, and I was a writer without a forum. I wanted nothing more than to recycle my hurt into something useful—to talk to people about empowering themselves and making proactive choices for their well-being. And I was armed with countless journals full of type A–organized lists of lessons. I wanted to believe that all my past hurt and ill health had evolved as precursors to this opportunity to do good in the world—that everything that came before had a clear and useful purpose involving my helping people, not fearing them. And let's call a spade a spade—it wasn't entirely a selfless act. I wanted to head to California on an adventure that would make me feel proud of my journey thus far. I imagined it would be wonderfully harmonizing after years of carrying shame in every crevice of my being.

I was hired as an alternate, in case someone had to drop out. I don't know if it was my honesty in sharing my struggles, my passion for helping people, or my desperation, but I did leave New York City with a job. Someone had to walk the Iams spokesdog along different parts of the journey (as with any event, Steps Across America had an interesting collection of sponsors and corporate goals), and that person, they decided, would be me.

But I couldn't ride the tour bus since the manager was allergic to dogs, and I had to book my own hotels since the group wouldn't always be staying at pet-friendly places. I wasn't required to be at any of the tour's events, and I wasn't allowed to blog. To me, this all sounded like another three months of isolation, with a massive canine dependent. I wouldn't be part of the group; I wouldn't get to share stories with other people who had felt powerless to take control over their lives; and I wouldn't get to make pithy observations online, catapulting me to instant web-celeb status.

That is exactly how I whined about it to my family, right before I hopped off my soapbox and realized the gift I'd been given. I was being paid more than the walkers because of the added responsibilities, and I had abundant free time while crossing the country in a rented vehicle I didn't have to pay for. In the weeks leading up to the tour, I called dozens of schools and hospitals to see if I could speak to girls about loving themselves and their bodies. I had a story to share about learning to value and take care of yourself, and fate had handed me an even better situation than I originally signed up for. I could book my own gigs, on my own terms, with school-aged girls who may not have known how amazing and valuable they were—how worthy of love, acceptance, and happiness. Of course, many of the people I contacted respectfully declined my offer, but some did not.

What's a more productive use of our energy—searching for meaning outside ourselves or creating meaning within ourselves? //

Whenever motivational speakers came to my elementary school back in the day, it always took me a while to warm up to them. At first I felt awkward and uncomfortable jumping into immediate intimacy with a stranger, and then there was the obligatory mocking between friends, communicated with eye rolls and giggles. School doesn't always feel like the safest environment to pin your heart to your sleeve or take a stand against immaturity. For this reason, I always understood when the girls I was now presenting to seemed distracted or resistant at the beginning of a session. They didn't know me; they didn't ask me to come; and they may or may not have been able to relate to the loneliness and low self-esteem I had developed at their age.

But every now and then, people completely defy expectations. The girl who did that for me appeared to be about twelve, and she had burn scars on both her face and her arms. She sat right in the front row during my fifth talk—no shying toward the back for her. She wore a short-sleeved shirt, which made sense considering the heat but felt to me unimaginably brave for a young girl who had been mutilated in a fire. She made eye contact with me immediately and seemed to comprehend a meaning behind my words that I hadn't even known to give them.

I told a story about my junior high years, exploring all the ways I learned to hate myself once it seemed like everyone else did. I talked about pressure and judgment, and how they can convince us there's something wrong with us. I explained that no one deserves to be mistreated, and that if we don't speak out, we might slowly start to believe otherwise. I talked about our differences—how kids can be cruel, especially when our bodies are changing, but we don't have to be defined by other people's perceptions. I'd given this same talk several times before, but somehow the trials and tribulations of puberty seemed insignificant considering the irreversible body transformation that the one particular girl staring at me had endured.

At the end, right after I said that we are all imperfect and yet we all deserve to be happy, I asked if anyone had any questions. That's when she raised her hand and asked, "Do you think bad things happen for a reason?" I couldn't help but wonder if what she was *really* asking was whether or not she somehow deserved her scars. I didn't have any definitive answer but, more important, I felt that what I thought didn't really matter. Regardless of what had happened or what she believed, she was choosing to be boldly herself—and during what has to be one of the most challenging times of a young girl's life. Whatever she told herself to make sense of her experience, wherever she'd learned to find strength and live with such an inspiring sense of presence, her own answer was something worth holding on to.

So I answered as honestly as I could: "I have no idea. But I know we can find a reason to use things that happen for good, and I know it feels good to focus on that."

Though we often look for significance in the face of tragedy, it's not just when we have trouble accepting life that we clutch to the idea of fate. I recently watched a documentary about lottery winners called *Lucky*. A couple won more than $110 million on a day when a detour brought them to a store they didn't usually patronize. The wife commented that it had to be fate—they were in just the right place at just the right time, though it was completely coincidental that they ended up there. But then that brings up the question: Why would they specifically be meant to win millions and another couple who took a detour to die in an accident? Why would some people be meant to have great fortune and others to know great hardship?

Here's a more interesting question: if a belief helps us find use in both good fortune and hardship, then does it matter whether it's true?

German philosopher Friedrich Nietzsche wrote about *amor fati*, Latin for "loving one's fate." The idea suggests seeing everything that happens in life as beautiful and good. A century earlier, in his book *Candide*, Voltaire proposed we *don't* live in the best of all possible worlds, but perhaps we needn't concern ourselves with that and instead should focus on the tasks in front of us—or "cultivate our own garden." I'll admit to enjoying these philosophies if for no other reason than that my mind likes to play with ideas, but I can see value in both perspectives. It's also clear to me that where we place our belief will influence our attitude, our sense of personal power, and, accordingly, our experience of life.

With this in mind, I asked on Twitter, "Does everything happen for a reason?"

Our choices make things happen

Everything happens, not for a reason, but from our decisions. ~@TheCatAndTheKey

Things happen as a consequence of the reason. ~@interrabang

Everything happens for a reason, but you have to understand that you are this only one making things happen. ~@Jimenix

The only reason things happen is due to our actions and mentality that we put into the world. Not of a greater being. ~@freckledjess

Everything happens for a reason if you choose it to be so. If you do, life becomes full of meaning, wonder, and growth. ~@Nirvana_Mamma

Do we have free will or is there something external guiding our choices and actions? Is there some type of cosmic plan leading us through specific experiences to a predetermined destination, or are our decisions our only road map? Does brain activity influence what we do before we're consciously aware of the choices we'll make? Are there other unconscious factors at play? Recent research has raised those questions, and one philosopher received $4.4 million to look into them.

As of January 2010, Alfred Mele, a professor at Florida State University, is spearheading a four-year exploration into free will that considers philosophy, science, and religion. Mele made an interesting observation when discussing the project, as reported on the FSU website:

"If we eventually discover that we don't have free will, the news will come out and we can predict that people's behavior will get worse as a consequence. We should have plans in place for how to deal with that news."

Past studies seem to indicate that people act aggressively and dishonestly when we believe we don't have free will, perhaps because there's a lot less guilt and fewer moral implications when we consider that maybe a decision isn't entirely in our own hands. Which is more useful: to believe we are in complete control and then make more positive choices, or to accept that we're powerless to fate and then leverage that to excuse bad behavior?

A few years back, I went on a date with a recovering alcoholic. Let's call him Rob. He told me the disease was in his blood, as his father was an alcoholic. I figured it was likely more environmental than genetic, but regardless, it made sense that to some extent alcoholism was in his future from a very young age. I admired that he made this early admission instead of sticking to his well-crafted personal elevator pitch, like a lot of us do on first dates. I also appreciated that he made it abundantly clear he never wanted to get married or have kids. It's a lot easier to have the "let's be friends" talk when you never really considered going beyond it. So we became friends—good ones.

> **W**e are the ones making the choices, and regardless of everything that influences them, we're the ones who need to be accountable. **"**

This might be why, a few weeks later, he felt comfortable enough to tell me that he had to register as a sex offender for sleeping with his adopted teen cousin. She had consented, according to Rob, but she was underage. Later I learned a second, even more disturbing story that still haunts me to this day: I have to imagine that Rob's younger sister, who couldn't have been more than five when he fondled her in his adolescence, wasn't as willing a participant as his cousin. When he told me that he had been touched by his older sister as a toddler, I felt a combination of compassion and repulsion that challenged everything I had previously thought about understanding and forgiveness.

Nothing condones abuse, but when someone has been abused, does that provide a viable explanation for their actions? Was it possible Rob's older sister, who also had been molested by their father, was part of an irrepressible cycle, which continued with Rob as well? Were his childhood choices somehow inevitable? And if that was the case, at what point does an abused child who learns to abuse have to take responsibility and learn a different way?

We all have difficult things in our past. We've all been hurt on some level, though some of us in more appalling and reprehensible ways. None of us had perfect parents, though some of us knew more idyllic childhoods than others did. Everyone has a closet, and there are at least a few skeletons in all of them. But at some point, we all need to decide that no one else can dictate what we do. No one else can decide how we react to our feelings. No one else can choose whether we act on instinct or question whether those impulses are actually serving us and the people around us.

We are the ones making the choices, and regardless of everything that influences them, we're the ones who need to be accountable—at least to the best of our ability. Someone with Parkinson's doesn't choose to tremble and someone with schizophrenia doesn't consent to hallucinate. But when it comes to the everyday decisions we all face, we are in the driver's seat. And if we aren't fully, if Professor Mele finds something that challenges this line of thinking, if the studies suggest a future where personal responsibility becomes obsolete: it might be in our best interest not to know.

Take back your power to choose.

If you've assumed that you are powerless to create the life you really want:

Identify the ways in which you feel stuck. Do you feel like you have to work in the family business because it's what your parents planned for you? Do you believe you'll never find someone to love you because you think you're damaged? Do you feel like you can't be happy because you hurt a lot of people and deserve to be miserable because of that? Think of this as cause-and-effect thinking—you are assuming that a cause has to lead to a specific effect.

Continues

Recognize how you are creating a self-fulfilling prophecy. Realize that things aren't happening because of external factors—they are happening because of how you respond to those external factors. Because you won't confront your family, you're working in a business you don't love. Because you think people won't love you, you're pushing them away. Because you're judging yourself, you're leaving yourself no room to forgive yourself. Realize the power is in what you choose to do.

Make a different choice in this moment. This isn't major transformation—it's one choice, right now, to see things differently and take control of your experience today. It might mean volunteering somewhere to feel out what you enjoy beyond that family business. Or sharing a little of yourself with someone new, instead of assuming people believe you're damaged. Or doing one thing that makes you happy instead of thinking about your happiness as a long-term impossibility. You don't need to worry about forever; you just have to choose to use this moment to create the future, instead of letting the future create you.

The reason something happens isn't as important as what you do after it does

Everything happens is the reason. ~**@marqueb**

The reasons things happen don't matter so much as the reasons you react to them the way you do. ~**@d_cahill**

Things just happen with purposes and consequences. ~**@twiras**

It's more useful to find benefit than seek cause. ~@jesusina

Reasons why stuff happens are made up and also very powerful. So make up useful reasons that make you feel liberated and loved. ~@cathduncan

When we fixate on reasons, it's almost like we're looking for someone to blame, or at least to hold accountable. Instead of focusing our attention on accepting, healing, and moving on from our experiences, we get lost in a sea of whys, looking for some logic in the past. Researcher Carey Morewedge found that we're more likely to assign blame for bad things that happen than to offer praise for good things. She hypothesized that we do this because we can't predict and prepare to avoid unexpected negative occurrences, so we instinctively want to believe something external was responsible. It feels safer to understand a specific cause. Unfortunately, there isn't always someone or something to accuse; and searching for that can keep us stuck for a lifetime.

Y ou don't need to worry about forever; you just have to choose to use this moment to create the future, instead of letting the future create you. //

Psychologists have also suggested that people are less likely to play the blame game if we're prone to finding the good in a situation. When we can see something as useful, it's easier to let go of that thing's bad parts and move on. It's empowering to imagine that, whatever happened, we can grow and prosper for having gone through it. If we're more apt to wallow in the unfairness of it all, we'll probably feel infuriated and want a target to receive that rage. What's more, we very well may get trapped there in that place of indignant self-pity. The moment we decide that something is inherently bad and that we are victims, our judgment starts a cycle of negative emotions. It's difficult to let go of anger and bitterness when we're convinced that we're justified in holding on to them.

The alternative is to focus on what we can do once something happens that we can't explain. It will naturally take time to get to that place—and we're allowed to take that time. Just like we go through seven stages of grief when someone dies, we need to follow a process to come to terms with other difficult changes. We need to allow ourselves to feel. At some point, however, we need to learn, grow, and choose to let it all go. As Ajahn Chah said, "If you let go a little, you will have a little peace. If you let go a lot, you will have a lot of peace." Part of that letting go is being accountable.

In the same *Discovery News* article where I first learned about Morewedge's blame research, writer Teresa Shipley referenced the Gulf of Mexico oil spill that happened on April 20, 2010. An explosion on a drilling rig for the BP oil company caused the largest oil spill ever—roughly 185 million gallons of oil when all was said and done. Investigations have revealed that workers on the rig felt hesitant to report safety violations, and further examination showed that equipment on the rig hadn't been inspected since 2000—even though it should be checked every three to five years. These reports, among others, came after Texas Governor Rick Perry suggested the oil spill might have been an act of God. He spoke in favor of continued drilling and said, "From time to time there are going to be things that occur that are acts of God that cannot be prevented."

There is a difference between an inexplicable tragedy, like a seven-year-old dying of natural causes, and a human-made mistake. Sometimes there are no answers, no matter how desperately we want to understand. But other times we needn't look any further than our own choices to explain the things that happen in our lives. In being honest with ourselves and acknowledging our humanity— the inevitability that we will make mistakes, both minor and major—we have immense power. We can't ever go back and change what happened. We can't un-spill the oil. The teens who relentlessly harassed their gay peers until they chose to commit suicide can't un-torment them. My cousin, who killed a man while driving under the influence, can't un-drink-and-drive. And the rest of us can't change the consequences of their actions by judging, berating, or ostracizing them. We can, however, learn.

We can learn to take better care of our earth—that we can't expect to deplete all of our natural resources, particularly not with an eye on cost-efficiency, if we want to protect our planet for future generations. We can learn to take better care of each other—that we need to offer compassion, understanding, and love if we want to live in a compassionate, understanding, and loving world where people don't hate and hurt each other. We can learn to take better care of ourselves—that what we put into our bodies and what we do in response to our feelings create a ripple effect for our future beyond a moment of instant gratification.

We won't always make the best choices, but we can keep learning to make better ones. The beautiful thing about life is that we have the ability to do things differently from one day to the next. We have the power to choose what we think and what we do. We have the choice to move on—even from the experiences we can't understand—with a determination to do good in the world. We can bounce back from any mistake and take the lesson to do something positive.

The reason may or may not be clear. Regardless, we can grow and, in doing so, change the world.

Let go of the need to place blame.

If you've been playing the victim in life:

Recognize blames that you've been holding on to. It may sound like this: Nothing good happens for me because I have bad luck. People don't like me because of my disability. I'll never get healthy because of my genetics. It's the government's fault that I'm on welfare. Whom or what do you often blame for the things that you wish didn't happen to you?

Turn a constructive finger at yourself. The point isn't to blame yourself— it's to take responsibility for your part in what happened so that you can make a positive adjustment in the future. Did your negative thinking create that "bad luck" by limiting the risks you took? Is your attitude about your disability pushing people away? Are you using your genetics as an excuse not to exercise?

Use what you learn—today. Once you take responsibility for your part, you can now decide how to move forward in a way that sets you up for a better result in the future. For example, in realizing that your negative thinking is creating your bad luck, you can now identify and reframe negative thoughts when they hold you back. You can challenge limiting beliefs and push yourself to do things differently. It's not about blaming anyone—including yourself. It's about letting go of bitterness related to something or someone else's role in what happened and empowering yourself to do something useful.

Sometimes we need to accept without needing to understand

Things happen due to the randomness of things, which ego-centered want to be special/unique humans have such a hard time with. We are all random links. ~**@wolforcaeagle**

It's what people say when something they can't understand happens. ~**@TEDDYMEISTER**

We may be able to sometimes find direction in things that happen, but it doesn't all happen for a reason. ~**@smola04**

People who look for reason in everything that happens become neurotic and superstitious. Life is about living. ~**@rcannon100**

There is order in randomness; we have to make sense of the chaos. ~**@sleepspell**

Without some greater understanding of why things happen—some idea of why we're here, why we're challenged, and why we eventually leave this world at a time that inevitably feels too soon—it can all seem somewhat pointless. Without a clear sense of purpose, actions seem arbitrary. When we don't feel a sense of universal order, everything feels unpredictable and frighteningly chaotic. Much like we needed stability as kids, we look for the same sense of constancy and security in adulthood. It's why studies show that people who have a clear sense of purpose report a greater sense of well-being than do people who don't. A guiding plan gives us a reason to go on.

Back then when we were kids, as much as we needed consistency, we also liked to test and push boundaries. We wanted to feel safe and secure within our environment, but we also wanted to see just how far we could go—exactly how much power we had to get the things we wanted. It's largely the same in adulthood. We crave the familiar but fantasize about the unknown. We fight for a sense of order, the perfect routine in the perfect job, only to then wonder what else is out there.

Life is a constant dance between wanting and resisting comfort. It's unlikely we'll ever relinquish the need to question, challenge, and want things. That's not to say we have to drive ourselves mad obsessing over things we can't explain or fester in discontent over everything that's lacking. Maybe the nature of things—the uncertainty, the impermanence, and that eternal sense of longing—is actually working in our favor. Maybe embracing the chaos and acknowledging that there are some things we can't control can actually be beneficial.

In their book *Seven Life Lessons of Chaos: Timeless Wisdom from the Science of Change*, John Briggs and F. David Peat suggest we can learn, grow, and prosper by accepting the randomness of life. For starters, our unpredictable world allows abundant opportunity for creativity. When we're less confined by perfectionism and rigid views of how things should be, we're better able to let our creations unfold before us. That random brushstroke from when you tripped while painting might be the start of an even greater masterpiece. The same theory translates into the workplace, where innovation tends to come from chaos and self-organization, not inflexible, overly bureaucratic structures. People often discover the best ideas when allowed to follow our own process.

Embracing chaos also shades the world a whole new level of beautiful, when you consider that every tree, every leaf, every snowflake, every cloud is similar to others but unique, with an infinite number of subtle nuances. And then there's the natural conclusion that we are fractally connected to each other and the universe at large. We may not be in total control, but we don't need to be. We are part of something, whether we fully understand it or not.

> **W**e can't change the nature of things, but we **can** change how we interpret it. "

If we choose to accept the world as it is, we have limitless opportunities for newness and excitement, unbridled by all the fears that keep us clutching at a greater sense of control. As a recovering perfectionist, type-A control freak, I understand the instinct to fight this. I know I feel alive and sublimely happy when spontaneity leads me on an adventure I didn't know to crave, but that's not always what happens when I let go. To the same degree uncertainty can be exciting and fun, it can be terrifying and painful. There is never any guarantee that an event will unfold exactly as we planned it—and no matter what religious or spiritual beliefs we adopt, there's no clear answer as to whether or not what happens will mean anything beyond the fact that it happened.

Roughly two years ago, Ehren took me on our second date, which started with a nosedive out of a tiny plane from thirteen thousand feet in the air. I'd mentioned casually on our first date that I had always wanted to go skydiving, which I did—someday. It didn't seem like the best second date plan, since it could entail tears and incontinence (luckily only the former was true). But I wanted to do it. I'd told him I wanted to do it, he'd done it before, and I wanted to prove to myself that I could.

Before he picked me up that day, I tweeted about my plans, and someone sent me a link about skydiving fatalities. I already knew it was possible that something could go wrong, but it seemed unlikely until I saw the cold hard facts. Suddenly I felt legitimately concerned my parachute might malfunction and send me plummeting to certain death—and how completely senseless. People might justify it by saying it was my time, or it was God's plan. But what if my death meant nothing more than that it's dangerous to hurl your body out of a plane? That no matter how controllable a situation may seem, things sometimes happen without any reason beyond the literal cause?

I made the jump that day—after leaving a note letting my family members know I loved them, just in case. I pushed myself to go, despite my fear and instinctive resistance, because it wasn't just a choice to impress my boyfriend-to-be. It was a choice to let go—to take a risk, feel alive, trust the system created to protect me, knowing it isn't infallible, and then accept the consequences of fully living. Every day is uncertain; even the least risky choices can lead to accidents for which no speculative reason will seem sufficient. We just can't know what the future holds, and fixating on that or clutching to comforting illusions won't change that. We can't change the nature of things, but we *can* change how we interpret it.

We can choose not to board the plane for fear of turbulence, lightning, or any other unpredictable force of nature, or we can recognize that sometimes, even the weather forecast is wrong,and it's worth the risk of what might be to soar among the chaotically beautiful clouds.

Embrace the chaos of life.

If you've been stressing out about chaos and uncertainty:

Learn to recognize when you know all you can. To some degree you can manage uncertainty by learning and making educated decisions, but there are always going to be variables you didn't know to plan for. No decision is 100 percent risk free, and you need to embrace that or you'll spend your whole life clinging to what feels safe, only to one day realize that nothing is. Instead of paralyzing yourself because of the things you don't know, empower yourself when you feel you know all you can, aware that, whatever happens, you can make the best of it.

Recognize the value in not knowing. It's human instinct to want to understand, but maybe the point isn't to have all the answers—maybe it's the experience of exploring the uncertainty and chaos. Because we don't know, we create, we innovate, we explore together. We write books. We make art. We make films. We design. We code. We invent. We find new ways to piece together the knowns and the unknowns to give life to new ideas.

Find your creative outlet. On her website *CreativityAtWork.com*, creativity and innovation consultant Linda Naiman suggests, "To make the most of chaos, look for patterns and connections between disparate data to formulate innovative ideas." What do you do with the patterns you identify? Do you write about them? Photograph them? Video them? Instead of trying to control everything to feel a sense of order, identify how you can take the disorder to create something useful and beautiful.

We are part of something greater than ourselves

Life's events play off one another, like the moon and the waves. ~@bjr71190

In nature, all things happen for a reason; reason constrained by reactions, time, and space. ~@quietman1920

If everything in life didn't happen for a reason, then what would be the point? ~@Richyboy81

Everything is energy. Things happen in the order they are supposed to in accordance with the energy flow surrounding them. ~@debismyname

It could take a day to months to years to figure out why something transpired how it did, but it was meant to occur. ~@jillianscrazy

You may be wondering how I can write an entire section on why things happen and only vaguely mention religion. How can I possibly address causes without exploring the various creation stories and offering due respect to a creator? Or, as someone who writes frequently about Buddhist ideals, how can I have discussed cause and effect without writing an in-depth treatise on energy and karma?

The only thing that I know for certain is that I do not know. I don't know in what literal way we're all connected. I don't know if there is a God or how to define that being.

I don't know if any creation story is even close to accurate. I don't know if we have souls or spirits, and whether or not they are all made from the same essence. I don't know if we exist beyond the experience we have on earth. I have no idea if we are all drops in the Universal ocean or if our individual consciousnesses are all pieces of one higher consciousness. If I wrote a blog on all the things that I don't know, I would have sufficient content to write every day for the rest of my life, and still not cover everything.

I suspect this is true for people in general: no matter how much we learn, there will always be a vast body of knowledge we not only don't have but also aren't equipped to understand. Living on earth, we see the effect, but can't pinpoint a cause, no matter how sure we are that something makes sense. There are answers out there, but that doesn't change the fact that we don't know them. In my eyes, it's far more valuable for us to come together in our common ignorance over the things we can't yet prove than it is to separate ourselves through assumed knowledge. The thing about beliefs is that they are not always facts, regardless of how comforting or plausible they may seem—and even if the majority of people believe them.

When I was fifteen years old, I was confirmed in the Catholic church wearing a pentagram. In retrospect, I realize this was blatantly disrespectful, regardless of what I may have believed at the time. Back then, it felt imperative that I do this. A year earlier, after getting my tarot cards read at a Boston psychic shop, I decided to become a Wiccan. Organized religion had never resonated with me, and I didn't know that I was willing to put my faith in anything I couldn't prove. I knew that Wicca was a New Age spiritual discipline that honored both gods and goddesses and that Wiccans believed they could create change in the world by working with energy and nature. I'd also seen a lot of practitioners wearing gorgeous velvet capes and participating in highly theatrical rituals. I figured if I was going to arbitrarily choose beliefs, they might as well involve magic and costumes.

I suggested to my family that I should skip the confirmation since I didn't actually want to take the sacrament, but that wasn't an option at the time. I won't blame my parents for this, because they were clearly doing what they thought was best. Back then, I didn't feel quite that way. Maybe it was my raging teenage hormones, residual angst, or just plain defiance, but I felt the need to make a strong point that day: I wouldn't be told what to believe or what my life means. I would not accept an explanation for life based on what other people agree sounds conceivable. If people wanted me to respect their beliefs—to allow them an answer that makes sense through their perceptions—they needed to do the same for me. I needed the freedom to understand how we are all connected, however it made sense to me. Ironically, in making that point, I failed to consider the impact it would have on some of the people I'm connected to. I wanted the most soothing possible answer, and I was willing to hurt people to own it.

It wasn't until years later, when I considered that maybe none of us are right, that I felt truly connected to everyone. That's something we all have in common: we all want to understand why we're here and why things happen. We all live in an uncertain world, and when we find an explanation that feels reassuring and empowering, we want to share it and even fight for it. We all want to believe there's some greater purpose—that we are not alone, but are, in fact, part of something larger than ourselves. Call it global consciousness, call it Universal energy, call it God—every religion revolves around it like the earth around the sun. Just like we want to be loved by each other, we want to know some higher power loves and looks out for us—the ones who are still here *and* the ones who have passed.

We can clutch at the things we'd like to believe, fighting each other for finding different theories more credible, or we can decide it's more important to be peaceful than right. We can desperately seek explanations for everything, using our energy to understand the bigger cause, or we can be the causes that create the effects we'd like to see in the world.

Does everything happen for a reason? Of course it does—lots of reasons. But the reasons don't matter anywhere near as much as what we do with what happens.

HAPPINESS

WHAT DOES IT
TAKE TO BE HAPPY?

They say sex sells, but it's nothing compared to happiness.

The happiness industry has exploded in recent years. According to a November 3, 2010, article on *PsychologyToday.com*, there were fifty books on happiness released in the year 2000 and four thousand published in 2008. Everywhere you look you see websites, blogs, articles, movies, documentaries, classes, e-courses, and seminars about finding happiness and holding on to it. We retain therapists to explore our unhappiness and ways to solve it. We hire life coaches to make detailed road maps that will lead us toward unadulterated bliss. We blog about it, tweet about it, hope for it, dream about it, look for it, plan for it, work toward it, analyze it, and all the while, have only a vague idea what it actually looks or feels like.

We compare ourselves to other people—their jobs, their families, their adventures, their relative freedom from the responsibilities that tie us all down—and plot to have what they have. Somewhere in the desiring, acquiring, and having, there has to be an answer, right? If only you get the promotion, you'll be happy. If only you find the right relationship, you'll be happy. If only you find your purpose, you'll be happy.

We read the latest in happiness research and measure ourselves against the findings, wanting to believe there's a concrete answer but suspecting happiness is best understood in experience, not analysis. I know I've been there. If goals are supposed to make you happy, I wondered, why do I feel so stressed and overwhelmed in the process? If the key to happiness is to focus more on experiences than on possessions, why do I sometimes miss out on my experiences by dwelling on the past, worrying about the future, and fearing the way I'll feel when the experience inevitably comes to end?

Why do we make happiness so exhausting?

Back when I first lived in San Francisco, about a year after I left New York City, I enrolled in a weekend-long personal development seminar touted as the last such course you'd ever need to take. To be honest, I felt a little resistant to that idea, but not for any sane reason. If I didn't keep reading self-help books, studying happiness, and stressing about my ability to apply what I learned, how else would I distract myself from myself?

I'd just lost my first writing job, which I got the day after I moved to the Bay Area. Truthfully, I was glad they laid me off. Back then, I never felt as free as when someone told me they weren't going to depend on me anymore. I didn't want to find another job or even stay in California. I wanted to go back on the road with a promotional tour, like the Steps Across America gig and others I'd done prior. Living out of a suitcase, developing relationships that spanned two days at most with housekeeping staff and waiters, I felt safe.

I told my San Francisco roommate, who had also moved around a lot, that I'd given it a good try and I was ready to move on. She encouraged me to push through to the other side. She knew it felt exciting, adventurous, and yet somehow safe to run away. She knew it felt uncomfortable to stay in one place. What she didn't know was what was on the other side of that discomfort—what it might feel like to move through the resistance, let ourselves go through the feelings, however messy they might be, and then see what happens as a result.

I would sooner have stranded myself on a deserted island with an anthropomorphized volleyball than risk being hurt in real relationships. I would have preferred to not own anything or have any financial obligations rather than to trap myself in a choice that might not be good enough. And it was far more my style to quit a job after a couple months than stay seven and get laid off. But I was too damn competitive to do what I'd always done. If *she* could put down roots, find a niche, and try to be happy, then damn it, I could, too.

I grabbed my cheap, old-school cell phone and signed up for the seminar. I was willing to do the work and write the check if it meant I could learn to be happy. It hurt a little putting out the $495, but I figured what the hell—I spent $700 on bliss for two homeless strangers. Wasn't my happiness worth as much?

The course involved three twelve-hour days, an instructor who looked like Sally Jessy Raphael, and a series of lessons that appeared to be paraphrased from the best self-help books ever sold. Over the course of that draining long weekend, I saw a middle-aged man break down in tears, acknowledging his alcoholic father did his best; I watched a tightly wound twentysomething convulse when Sally Jessy called her out on being selfish and responsible for the drama in her family; and I sat enthralled as, one by one, dozens of exhausted people accepted responsibility for their happiness and had life-changing transformations, as visibly evident as a mass exorcism.

Why do we make happiness so exhausting? "

They say that a lot of cult members have a hard time walking away even after they've accepted they're up to their ears in no good, because it's too hard to admit they made a massive error in judgment. It's basically the sunk cost principle—that once you've put a lot of time or money into a choice, you'd rather knowingly keep doing something fruitless, senseless, or unfulfilling than cut your losses and start over. That's kind of what happened in that moment for me. I *didn't* transform—but I had paid for transformation, so transformation I would get.

I pretended I'd never heard that unhappiness comes from hanging on to the past, victimizing ourselves, and interpreting things based on our perceptions and judgments, and I visualized what it might look like if I suddenly awakened after a lifetime of living numb. Then I broke down in tears—deep, gasping, lip-quivering wails. I trembled. I shook my head, as if in disbelief and awe over the sudden leap in personal evolution. I put my hands in the prayer position as if recognizing the divine in the ordinary. Somewhere between sobbing and spewing incoherent confessions about the error of my ways, something strange happened: I felt vulnerably authentic.

The same ideas I'd read dozens of times in countless different ways suddenly felt more meaningful than ever before. I knew them inside and out—not just intellectually but also in my blood, in my bones, in my flesh. Gutting myself in front of a room full of strangers was infinitely more satisfying than holing up with a book, especially now that I was doing it as me, not some character I chose to play. After admitting that I didn't want to be unhappy, that I wanted to love myself, and that I didn't want to run away anymore, I completely exposed myself with one final admission: "I don't want to be scared of you." It's draining and depressing to suspect everyone wants to hurt you, but that's the way I lived—terrified of everyone I met or might meet.

In that moment, I wasn't scared. I was so involved in this embarrassingly raw experience that I didn't have a chance to judge it—or anything else. Immersed in our collective understanding, present in my body, and naked in their sight line, I felt that happiness was possible. If I quieted the voice in my head—the inner tormenter that analyzed ad nauseum—and let myself be part of the world around me, I could be eternally happy. All I had to do was stop my mind. Day in and day out. Indefinitely.

The next day, I walked down the street in complete connection to the present moment. I heard every sound—birds flying overhead, the low hum of construction equipment in the distance, children giggling as they ran through fields of dandelions just beyond the horizon (or maybe it was the housing projects). I saw the sights more vividly than ever before, when I multitasked walking and overthinking—who knew there were leaves on the tree near my house? I smelled every scent and nuance of scent.

For a while, everything was perfect—until I ended my pleasant, responsibility-and-people-free spring walk and planted myself back into reality. With a lot of people who *weren't* disarmingly vulnerable. With or without them surrounding me, my life was still my life. I still didn't have a job. I still had rent far higher than any I'd ever paid. I still had a world waiting to be filled with people, interests, and at least some things. And I still had an inner voice that I'd have to continue learning to tame for the rest of my life. What I *didn't* have was $495—and for a minute I was pissed.

"The industry preys on the weak!" I told my sister. "They lure in the most vulnerable people—people dealing with heartbreak, loss, disappointment, and emptiness—and make everything sound so deceptively simple. *Of course* you experience gut-wrenching catharsis when you're sleep-deprived and desperate for an answer."

Somewhere between feeling indignant and scheming about the exposé I'd write for *Time* magazine, I realized how ridiculous it all was. I'd spent $495 to learn how to be happy and then felt angry when I realized my money didn't hire someone else to live in my head.

In the end, that's what it comes down to. No amount of learning, striving, or fighting can change the fact that only we can choose to be happy. Only we can decide what to do with our energy, time, and money, and only we can decide whether to fight our reality or let go and be present within it.

Only we can choose the relationships, the jobs, the homes, the cities. Only we can fill our hours. And only we can give ourselves permission to enjoy them. There will always be the possibility of something else, something on the other side of wherever you are. But the only opportunity to feel joy is here and now because tomorrow we'll be smack-dab in the middle of another here and now. There have been times when I've felt peaceful and content and I've wondered, *Is this all there is?* Like, maybe that was just the Two-Buck Chuck version of happiness, and there was Dom Perignon still out there to be tasted. In looking for some greater happiness, I completely disregarded how fortunate I was to be content. In dreaming of far worthier experiences, I forgot how much power I had to shape the present moment, whatever it entailed.

There's this man who works at the 7-Eleven near my old apartment. This little guy, with his colorful button-down shirt and funny-looking hat, made my day most mornings. Everytime I came in to get my coffee, he was either laughing or sharing a story about his day with a customer, using a voice so chipper it sounded like singing. At first I thought he was just putting on a good face, making the best of a tough situation. After all, he couldn't possibly enjoy working at a convenience store, right? Then I realized I was missing the biggest part of his appeal: he *does* enjoy his job, and that's why he seemed so happy—because he chooses to be. He chooses to engage with people. He chooses to smile. He chooses to see the moment as enough, regardless of what he might accomplish tomorrow.

We can, too.

"What does it take to be happy?" That is the next question I asked on Twitter.

The happiest people take responsibility for creating their own joy

Nobody can make you happy or unhappy. It is just you who allows them to do so. ~@Brenazet

Recognizing that happiness exists within; not in people, places, or things. ~@loilaing

Sometimes, it's as easy as just deciding to be happy, stop worrying, and enjoy your day more fully. ~@draona

It takes the personal realization that one's happiness is derived from within and not from without. ~@geoffreypelkey

I am the source of my own happiness. If I am happy, my experience of the world will be happy. ~@frankilus

If you're into happiness research, that ever-growing body of evidence that bliss is indeed a science, you've probably heard the phrase "positive psychology," coined by psychiatrist Martin Seligman in 2000. Previously, psychology focused on healing emotional and mental problems but didn't identify ways people without such conditions could thrive in life. It wasn't about happiness; it was about fighting depression, anxiety, and mental illness.

A big part of the posi-psy equation is the dichotomy of learned helplessness versus learned optimism. When you perceive that you don't have control in your situation—particularly when you believe you're somehow flawed or that your difficulties are permanent and inescapable—that's learned helplessness. It quite often leads to depression. Your parents and teachers likely had a lot to do with the way you perceive your circumstances and yourself. If your mother saw everything as a hopeless catastrophe and took everything personally, it's likely you developed the same type of thinking.

Learned optimism is the practice of challenging that self-talk that makes you feel trapped in a bad situation. It's about questioning what you believe about the things that happen—what you assume they mean—and then actively disputing those beliefs. Let's say you feel you've flubbed a job interview, and you instinctively believe that means you're incompetent and will never get a job. You could dispute those thoughts by reminding yourself this one job interview isn't a complete reflection of your talents, skills, and potential; just because you didn't get one job, that doesn't mean you're unemployable and destined to spend the rest of your life poor, alone, living in a van down by the river. One event that appears to be negative does not have to define you or limit your possibilities.

> **Y**ou're not just creating your own happiness.
> You're showing other people it's possible. "

If you do feel out of control in life—if you're at the mercy of your own self-inflicted victimization and not taking any active measures to change it—it's useless to suggest you create your own joy. Every time you put yourself in a situation where you might experience happiness, your thoughts will sabotage you. If the majority of your thoughts suggest you're doomed to a life of unhappiness, and that maybe you deserve it, you will feel anxious and incapable of creating or experiencing true joy.

In case it is not already abundantly clear, I'll tell you: I've been there before. In fact, I felt like this for the first twenty-two years of my life, and intermittently over the next nine years. I am by no means a complete optimist. There are still times when I judge myself in my head, as the architect of my own discontent. But I know whenever I do that I am consciously choosing not to be happy. We can only create the world we want to experience when we believe we can. We can only be proactive when we get out of our way.

There is someone I love who is painfully cruel to herself. It hurts to watch, partly because I know what it feels like, and partly because in acknowledging her learned helplessness, I am helpless. It doesn't matter how much I think I understand. It doesn't matter how confident I feel about the solution to her depression (she's tried every possible treatment). It doesn't matter how well I play amateur psychiatrist, or how many platitudes I can cram into one potentially motivating pep talk. It doesn't matter that I want her to be healed, if she isn't willing to heal herself. And that right there, I believe, is the hardest part of learned optimism. No matter how empowered we feel about creating and experiencing joy, we can't control the people around us. We can't ensure they'll fall in line with our plans. We can't make them love themselves. And if we want to keep being kind to ourselves, we can't follow their lead.

We can't give happiness to anyone else. But by nurturing our own thoughts, and sprinkling that sense of possibility in the world around us, we just might show them how things can be. When you choose to do the things you love, and to focus on how fortunate you are to be able to do those things; when you live your day with a sense of wonder, awe, and self-acceptance; when you let other people be a part of it— you're not just creating your own happiness: You're showing other people it's possible.

Practice learned optimism.

If you often feel a sense of helplessness:

Recognize pessimistic thinking patterns. Seligman identified four differences between optimists and pessimists: permanence, pervasiveness, hope, and personalization. When something that seems bad happens, do you instinctively feel that your life is permanently ruined? Do you feel helpless in every way, as opposed to feeling frustrated with just that one area of your life? Do you feel like the cause was something that's permanent—meaning, you're doomed to feel this way again? Do you tend to blame yourself?

Track your reactions for three days using the ABC model. If you recognized pessimistic tendencies, this is a simple way to start turning those around. A stands for *adversity.* B stands for *belief.* C stands for *consequences.* For example: The adversity might be that you failed your driver's test. The belief may be

Continues

that you're stupid and never do well under pressure. The consequence is that you get down on yourself, fail to schedule a new test, and feel depressed all day and night. Keep track of the minor adversities in your days. Then go back to your journal and categorize your pessimistic tendencies (i.e.: thinking that you never do well under pressure is permanence; feeling depressed all day is pervasiveness).

Start adding D and E to ABC. D stands for *disputation* and E stands for *energization.* When you encounter adversities going forward, dispute the beliefs with evidence to the contrary—so when you think, *I'm stupid and never do well under pressure,* remind yourself, *I'm not stupid—I excel at a lot of things—and I do really well under pressure when someone I love needs me.* Energization is the act of celebrating the positive feelings you've now created. This, in a nutshell, is Seligman's model for creating optimism, which will make it much easier to feel joy, even in the face of difficult circumstances.

Positivity is the key to happiness

You cannot change the world, so enjoy the little daily pleasures and you will be happy. ~**@MegametedK**

To be happy all you really need is a positive attitude and mindfulness. ~**@YouKnowJayCub**

All you really need to be happy is the right mindset. That determines how you handle everything in life, especially the lemons. ~**@JayeSN**

A complete disregard to all the bad things in life is all it takes. See everything for the good and put the bad to the side. ~@**Foggydoggg**

Real happiness is beyond all circumstances. Being happy is an effect from inside to outside, not the opposite. ~@**tatsushirou**

It's true: the glass *is* half empty.

I know that might sound odd coming on the heels of a section about learned optimism, but I believe in positivity that's hinged on reality—and the truth is, the glass is *both* half empty and half full. It isn't one or the other. Shakespeare wrote, "There is nothing either good or bad but thinking makes it so." The circumstances we experience happen, and then we decide what they mean. We decide what's good, what's bad, what's fair, and what's unfair.

Proponents of positive thinking suggest we should focus our interpretations on the good and the fair—always look for the silver lining in everything that happened, and reframe thoughts so it seems that everything occurs for our highest good. For a long time, this is precisely what I believed, until I realized I was thinking positively with an agenda. It wasn't simply about reframing what I perceived as bad so I could feel empowered and peaceful; it was about pretending I believed something good so that I'd look good—and in the process, hopefully propel myself to something better. Let's face it: that's what a lot of us associate with a positive attitude—the hope that it will attract conditions that we believe to be positive.

According to Barbara Ehrenreich, author of *Bright-Sided*, the ideology of positive thinking can seem to suggest that attitude is the ultimate predictor of what happens to us in life—as if her cancer diagnosis was something she brought on herself by not being upbeat. Ehrenreich also resents the idea that she should see cancer as some sort of gift. She cites a number of research studies, some suggesting that our positive-thinking culture has encouraged cancer patients to repress their real and totally normal feelings in the hope their attitudes can somehow heal their bodies—which can eventually leave them feeling like they have failed if the disease continues to spread. Essentially, this boils down to the law of attraction, popularized in the book *The Secret*. It's the idea that our inner world creates our outer world—that somehow we can think our way away from what we don't want and toward what we do. Implicit in this philosophy is that idea that we are the architects of our own health and disease.

What seems like a far more realistic thought is that our attitudes influence our physical health, but they are not the sole factors. And just like we can't completely control what happens with our bodies, we can't ever guarantee ourselves specific outcomes solely through positive thinking. Where positive thinking becomes a gateway to unhappiness is when we assume it will lead to specific results, and then put pressure on ourselves not only to suppress emotions and reframe thoughts but also to do so well enough that we get what we think we want.

The alternative is to choose positive thinking not because it will get us what we think we want in the future but because it, in itself, is what we want in the present. It just plain feels good to think empowered, self-affirming thoughts, as opposed to defeatist, depressing ones. Our thoughts affect our feelings and ultimately influence what we choose to do. In this way, when we focus on the positive, we're more likely to find ourselves in situations that feel good—not because we get exactly what we want but because we'll always be open to finding something worth having in what we get.

That being said, it also feels good to accept human nature rather than try to fight it, and it is inevitable that things are going to happen that we judge as bad. Denying this creates internal conflict and resentment. If you've just been raped, you have every right to feel bitter and angry for a while. If you've just lost someone you love, you have every right to grieve. The things you are thinking that might seem negative are totally healthy and normal. Allowing yourself to think them while you heal won't attract more tragedy. You are more powerful than you think, but not so powerful that every thought creates something in form. You don't need to repress your thoughts, label them, or replace them, or stress over your inability to find a more positive slant.

You just need to know that you are willing to heal and then take responsibility for creating a more peaceful space in your head—not just because it will attract what you want but also because you occupy that mental space all day every day. If it's persistently depressing and negative in there, of course you won't be happy. Of course you'll constantly fixate on all the things you want to attract to make you feel better about your life. If you're anything like me, you'll be looking for an escape from yourself.

Like anything in life, positive thinking can feel negative if you have unrealistic expectations of what it can do for you. It can't protect you from uncertainty and pain in life. And it can't change that some things won't ever seem good to you. What it *can* do is help you learn to feel good more often than not. In my book (which this is), *that's* happiness.

Practice realistic positive thinking.

If positive thinking has been feeling stressful for you:

Recognize if you're trying to suppress something painful with positivity. Are you ignoring what you really feel about something so that other people think you're being positive? Are you telling yourself to "suck it up" and focus on the good things, when what you really want to do is curl up in a ball and cry?

Give yourself a window of time to work through the feelings. Depending on what you're dealing with, you may need a large window and professional help. If it's a disappointment but not something traumatic, give yourself a window that your instincts say feels sufficient—a day, a week, whatever feels right in your gut. Then spend that time working through your feelings. Write about them. Express them through art. Communicate your feelings to another person if there needs to be some sort of confrontation. Do what needs to be done to eventually let go and move on.

When the window is over, identify something proactive you can do right now. Realistic positive thinking means you don't have to pretend that conditions you believe are negative are actually positive. If you don't feel like something is a blessing in disguise, it won't help you to pretend you do. Instead, shift your focus to how you can empower yourself now. So you lost your job, and you loved it. There's no denying that. But what's also true is that you can start researching other jobs today, and you may find one you'll love even more, if you're willing to believe that's possible. It doesn't change how you feel about what you lost or guarantee anything specific; it just illuminates possibilities and places you in the right mind-set to recognize and enjoy them.

Happiness is about being present

We find happiness only in the present moment. ~@LesleyAnnM

Focus on the activity and not the outcome. ~@ShennandoahDiaz

Happiness is being present, right here, in this moment. By grasping at what isn't, we invariably take for granted what is. ~@crazynessa524

To be happy is to be present at any given moment. Awareness of what you are doing is just as important as your next activity or chore. ~@lenidec

A mindful moment you take, you give yourself, perhaps by closing your eyes to see how much there is still to be thankful for. ~@hansoulkim

People are always telling each other to be mindful—to stop dwelling on the past and worrying about the future and instead dig our heels into the moment with awareness and gratitude. Though mindfulness is one of the cornerstones of Buddhism and other spiritual disciplines, it's not just gurus and yogis who recommend it. Business leaders suggest mindfulness as a means to access flow, that state when we're in the zone, doing our best work without distracting mental chatter. Psychiatrists advocate mindfulness as a solution for anxiety, pain, and depression. And scientists continue to study the effects of mindfulness on the brain and body, noting a host of physical benefits.

Yet even equipped with all this expert advice and neurological research, most of us still live our days at the mercy of our thoughts. Studies show that the vast majority of them center on stresses, insecurities, fears, and judgments, directed at both the world around us and ourselves. We analyze things that happen, creating stories about what they mean. We hold on to things that happened before, hoping the memories will protect us from pain in the future. And perhaps most stressful, we analyze life as we go, judging, assessing, and generally drowning the moment with our internal observations and self-critique.

Mindfulness can seem like an overwhelming proposition because we often don't embrace mindfulness mindfully. At least *I* didn't. When I first learned about meditation, yoga, and absorbing myself in the moment, particularly after I experienced how good it felt, I wondered if it was possible to maintain that permanently. Was it really a sustainable practice? Would I ever completely silence the voice in my head? In other words, could I get really good at being mindful? Could I learn to be in the present moment forever, so that tomorrow, and the next day, and the next day, I was living a fully present life? As the eternal queen of irony, I didn't realize that thinking about tomorrow's mindfulness completely defeats the purpose.

Trying to be mindful is one of the biggest obstacles to *being* mindful. When you try to be mindful, you analyze your actions, judge yourself for having thoughts instead of letting them pass, and question whether you're actually being mindful or if perhaps you're just going through the motions. When you *are* mindful, you stop thinking about what you're doing and thinking and use that energy instead to become fully conscious of your surroundings. The big difference is whether you become aware of your thoughts and then think about that awareness, or if you learn to quiet your thoughts and fully experience awareness.

You probably know where I'm going with this. This is the section where I *could* go into an advanced explanation of meditation, exploring the different styles and traditions and encouraging you to develop a disciplined practice that involves at least an hour a day of sitting in stillness. But I can't do that in good conscience because I don't do that. I am not a perfect meditator, and allowing myself not to be has been a powerful decision. I engage in deep-breathing exercises every morning, and I practice yoga regularly—sometimes more regularly than others. Sometimes I take long, slow afternoon walks, syncing my steps with my breaths, and sometimes I don't. That's what works for me, and that's what I'm willing to sustain. By not approaching meditation as a rigid, all-or-nothing proposition, I increase my odds of consistently doing the things that ground me in the moment—and accordingly, enhance my access to mindfulness.

We don't all have to run out and get the same cushion, or any cushion at all. We don't have to spend time in an ashram à la *Eat Pray Love* and gut ourselves, exploring every layer of resistance in a controlled group environment. We don't have to fast, or take vows of silence, or learn to balance on one foot, or learn the ancient art of tai chi, or start drinking loose-leaf tea while sitting cross-legged. These are all things we *can* do, and it might be smart to adopt some of these suggestions. But all that really matters is that we do something—whatever makes sense to us each individually—to foster present-moment awareness.

Even immersing yourself in activity you love can be meditative. Much like tai chi and yoga connect breath and movement, jogging, dancing, or even crocheting, getting lost in those repetitive motions, can be a meditative practice. If the end goal is to minimize negative, judging thoughts in order to experience the world with less resistance, the means is to quiet your thoughts on the whole. Any day you make the active choice to create a sense of inner calm, you increase your odds of noticing and experiencing all the beauty the world has to offer.

Cultivate mental quiet.

If racing thoughts are making it difficult to be fully present:

Use the one-hundred-breaths technique. In her *TinyBuddha.com* blog post "8 Ways to Make Meditation Easy and Fun," Goddess Leonie recommends counting breaths from one to one hundred. You might feel resistant at first, but you'll feel stiller and calmer with each passing breath. If you feel resistant, tell yourself it's just ten breaths. Most likely, it will start to feel good, which will encourage you to keep going.

Alternate nostril breathing. This is my breathing technique of choice. Use your left ring finger to hold down your right nostril. Inhale through the left nostril for four counts. Use your thumb to hold down your left nostril, and with both nostrils blocked, hold for four counts. Release your right finger and breathe out through your right nostril. Now start by breathing in through your right nostril and repeat the whole process. This is one set. Complete four to eight of them.

Practice mindfulness in a routine activity. Whether it's doing dishes, folding laundry, or mowing the lawn, decide to enjoy it instead of resisting it. Tune in to the sounds of birds outside your window or kids laughing down the street. Feel the physical sensations—the warm water, or the soft clothes, or the cool handle of the mower. Smell the lemon soap, the fabric softener, or the freshly cut grass. Tune in to all your senses and, in that moment, pretend that this is all that exists—only what you can perceive right now.

Get into the zone. Pick an activity you enjoy doing or want to learn to do—something that will consume all your focus, like practicing yoga, playing basketball, or even taking a beginner's class at trapeze school. When you immerse yourself in a physical activity, concentrating completely on what's going on in your body, you will naturally create a sense of inner clarity.

Happiness comes from focusing on others

Do something simple. Make your loved one smile. ~**@davidhepi**

To see the happiness of others indistinguishably as our own—that's happiness. ~**@AgaNY**

You'll be happy if you wish happiness for the others, if you do what you enjoy, and if you laugh. ~**@feboop**

Happiness comes from compassion and the choice to simply be happy. Recognize the beauty that constantly surrounds us! ~**@Nicholas_OSC**

One: Attain the simplest mind and higher self. Two: Attain appreciation for all events and things. Three: Help others attain one and two. ~**@zenfeed**

In *The Art of Happiness in a Troubled World*, the Dalai Lama suggests that extreme individualism can be a cause of unhappiness. When you're so self-reliant you shut other people out and spend more time pushing toward goals than enjoying the moment, you're bound to feel dissatisfied. We *need* meaningful face-to-face contact to feel engaged and fulfilled, not to mention balanced. Some cultures promote an individualist mind-set as the ultimate for success, which makes releasing that norm challenging. It's ingrained in us from a young age, when we first learn about materialism through commercials and we start connecting the dots between working, acquiring, achieving status, and experiencing joy.

The opposite isn't healthy, either; extreme socialist societies don't breed happy people. We need both a sense of independent identity and an understanding of our role in the larger picture. We need to realize that we have limitless possibilities for what we can create, achieve, and discover, but also know that what we do impacts the people around us, and that everyone benefits when we each choose to look out for each other. We need to know it isn't "me" versus "we"—we can have both.

It sounds so simple, and what a wonderful world that would be. If you've ever watched a young kid for any length of time, you've seen firsthand how freeing undiscriminating compassion and vulnerability can be. A three-year-old boy won't question Grandma's character when she overreacts to something small. He'll just run up and give her a marathon-long hug because hugs make *him* feel better when he's upset. A four-year-old girl wouldn't berate herself for crying in front of Uncle Mike, feeling scared he might judge her or use it against her later. She'd just let it all out, albeit with more arm flailing and gasping than her adult counterpart, and then assume Mike still loves her. There's nothing more liberating than truly believing other people are good and they aren't waiting to hurt you. There's nothing more comforting than accepting that you don't have to walk around in fear.

But that's something we often do as adults. We form tightly woven understandings of who we are based on past experiences, perceived strengths and weaknesses, desires, and fears, and then we hold on to those fragile concepts for dear life. We identify what we like and what we don't, what we believe and what we doubt, what we assume about other people and what we're not willing to believe—and then we fight for all of it. It's who we are, we imagine, and we won't let anyone question, offend, condescend, stifle, dispute, or threaten that in any way. We won't let other people make us feel inferior; we won't let them tell us we're wrong; we won't let them hold us back. We know who we are, and that's all that matters.

Sounds like a lot of empowering stuff, right? I used to think so. Then I started thinking about all that defensive self-talk. Why did I assume so many people wanted to question, offend, stifle, and dispute me? And why was I holding so tightly to my identity within the collective when I was willing and even eager to learn and grow, so long as I felt it was *my* choice and *I* was in complete control? Why do we repeatedly tell ourselves things that imply lots of other people will want to take something from us?

Think for a minute about the "us against the world" perspective. It's a popular anthem for the alone-together. Why be isolated and bitter about *them*—the people you don't know and don't trust, who will inevitably hurt you if you're not careful—when you can be bitter with another person who'd love to belong with you while fearing everyone else?

At a bitter time in my life, I felt incredulous when I read about love connecting the world. I thought it was the kind of thing you write when you're sheltered, tripping on acid, or being paid to sell a fantasy. Then I realized that I could be as cynical as I wanted to be if I was willing to trade happiness for being right about everyone else being wrong. *Or* I could consider the possibility that other people are just like me, and they wake up every day wanting the same things. They want to feel secure and happy. They want to feel accepted and understood—like people *get* them. They don't want to be judged by one mistake. And they still feel really good inside when someone gives them an honest, uncomfortably long hug—the kind that has no expectations or agenda other than to love.

Does focusing on other people make you happy? It depends on how you look at it. Other people can be a great distraction from your circumstances if you give them your attention for a while, but eventually you'll be back where you started. It's only when we appreciate that we truly are all in this together—in our desires, our fears, and our imperfections—and then give someone else the love we crave that our connections become a source of true joy.

Create a balance between *me* and *we*.

To create a sense of autonomy and belonging:

Recognize if you veer toward extreme individualism or constant connection. Do you tend to spend extended periods of time alone and avoid social situations? Do you close yourself off from other people, thinking that they might hurt you? Or, do you feel the need to always be doing something with other people? Does the thought of spending time alone make you feel anxious?

Identify fears that may be creating this imbalance. If you veer toward extreme individualism, you may be isolating yourself because you're afraid that other people will judge you, or that you won't achieve your goals if you don't focus on them 24/7. If you veer toward constant connection, you may be afraid that you'll feel something uncomfortable when you're not distracted, or that you'll somehow lose your friends if you're not around them all the time. Dig deep to identify whatever fears may be motivating you to do what you do.

Dispute the beliefs that cause the fears. If you're afraid people will judge you, remind yourself that this is not a fact. The alternative is that they may love you and fill your life with a sense of joy and connection. You'll only know if you put yourself out there. If you're afraid your relationships may suffer if you don't constantly tend to them, remind yourself that this is not a fact. If you take time to nurture your relationship with yourself, you'll ultimately have a lot more to bring to your relationships, which ultimately could make them stronger. You'll only know if you give yourself that space.

Create meaningful balance—starting today. Make a choice today to spend a little quality time with yourself, and a little quality time with other

Continues

people. *Quality* is the operative word here. Take a long walk alone to connect with your intuition, or grab your journal and go to the park. This is your time to tune in to the happiness you feel that doesn't require anybody else's involvement or approval. Then create at least a small window of time when you share happiness with another person or a group. Maybe it's a lunch where you catch up and share dreams, or it's an activity based on a shared passion. The point is to create the conditions within your day that allow you to feel both autonomy *and* a sense of belonging. Aim to do this, at least a little, on most days of the week.

Happiness is letting go of expectations and appreciating what you have

When you have nothing, want nothing, and need nothing, you are happy. ~**@rpvgriendt**

Happiness is learning to love what you have and not obsessing over what you don't have. ~**@unmemorablehero**

Let go of everything, for it is all impermanent! ~**@ryanlederman**

Recognize that you have everything you need to be happy right now. ~**@TheStephy_Chi**

Happiness comes from having good health, not desiring anything excessive other than good health, and being thankful for it. ~**@cyberfic**

You don't get the job. Your significant other leaves with no explanation. After years of hard work, you learn your business is about to go bankrupt. These are the blows that devastate expectations—some written in shorthand on a napkin, and others worn from years of revision. These expectations aren't the ones that fall off at the end of a day, like the compliments you anticipated on your hair but never received. These are the expectations wrapped up in hope that someday something will be exactly as you dreamed it.

They live in a different time when things are just right—when the world is fair and your affection is returned or your hard work pays off. But they're kind of like Jenga pieces. Even if you put them in all the right places, that doesn't change the risk inherent in the game. There are no guarantees in life, and sometimes even the best laid plans don't pan out. I don't mean this to sound cynical. This isn't me bemoaning the bleak reality of our existence, though I'm human, and sometimes it scares me how much is out of my control. But the reality is that tomorrow is most certainly uncertain and no matter how many expectations we form, it will come, it will go, and it will be what it will be. Somehow, accepting that makes the good things more valuable and the bad things less shocking.

The other day, a *TinyBuddha.com* reader wrote to me about our similarities. She is also from Massachusetts, she'd moved to California to pursue her dreams, and she too had a life that was nothing like she once imagined it. As a kid, she had assumed she'd be married with children and a successful career by age thirty. She was right—we do have a lot in common. If you'd told six-year-old me I'd be thirty-one, unmarried, without children, and still figuring out what I wanted to be when I grew up, I'd visualize my gray-haired self (because thirty is over the hill) eating cat food in a shack—the lowest of the low in my favorite girl-hood game, MASH.

And yet this single, childless, unwritten life is more fulfilling than I ever imagined it could be—partly because it lacks premature grays and Meow Mix and partly because younger me didn't know to expect the amazing possibilities I've created. That's the thing about expectations—they presuppose we know what's best for us. Sure, sometimes we think we know what we want, and maybe we do. We may even spend extensive time trying to attract those things through positive thinking, visualization, and other *Secret*-esque acts of willful manifestation. But when we attach ourselves to a specific tomorrow, we limit its potential.

My favorite book of last summer was *Sway: The Irresistible Pull of Irrational Behavior*. Throughout the book, Ori and Rom Brafman explain the psychology behind some of the illogical decisions we make on a day-to-day basis. Every section is fascinating, but one that really stuck with me dealt with our righteous commitment to seeing justice served. The authors reference a German research study where strangers were "partnered up" anonymously and kept in separate rooms, with $10 to split between them. One participant in each pair got to decide how the money would be split, and the other had to decide whether or not to accept the offer. If he or she refused, neither would get to keep any money. You might assume that any offer would be good since some money was better than none, but most of the time, when the partner with the power decided to give himself a higher share, the other person rejected the offer because it wasn't fair. The results remained the same when the researchers repeated the experiment with $100 instead of $10.

Researcher Joseph Henrich conducted this same study at UCLA using $160, what a student might earn in three days of work. Most students decided to split the money because it was fair, but they also admitted they wouldn't have accepted any less than 50 percent if the tables were turned. Henrich finished his research by bringing this experiment to Machiguenga, an isolated section of the Amazon. Unlike in the other experiments, these people were willing to accept any offer because it was money they wouldn't have otherwise had—and they actually understood the reasoning or impulse if the person who divvied it up chose to keep a larger share. Instead of assuming they were entitled to half, they felt grateful to have gotten any at all.

This may have seemed like a non sequitur, but it's quite relevant. We carry around a lot of beliefs about how things should work in the world, and sometimes they blind us to the beauty in what is. In assuming life is unfair for giving us 30 percent of what we think we deserve, we forget how fortunate we are to be given anything at all.

Today, exactly as it is, imperfect, unbalanced, and potentially overwhelming, is the perfect day to feel happy. The feeling won't be permanent; nothing is. So take the pressure off of holding on to the moment, expecting it should last forever, or that it will hurt when it's over. Instead, give yourself permission to enjoy and appreciate what is. In this moment, it's enough.

Shift from expectation
to appreciation
(without getting complacent).

If you find yourself dwelling on what's fair and always feeling a sense of lack:

Create a daily gratitude practice. This might mean writing down three things you appreciate in a gratitude journal every morning, or it could mean telling at least three people daily how much you value something they've done for you (in person or even online). The point is to program your mind to recognize all the positive things you have in your life at any moment. This doesn't guarantee that you'll attract all the positive things you want in abundance, but it makes it more likely that you'll focus on the things that really matter and feel a sense of peace with what is right now.

Instead of bemoaning what's not fair, commit to identifying how you're fortunate. If your unethical colleague is making more money than you, remind yourself that you're fortunate to have strong values that will ensure your success never feels empty. If your wife cheated on you but somehow cleaned up in the divorce, remind yourself that you're fortunate to be out of an unhealthy relationship with someone who is so clearly unhappy in life. This doesn't mean you shouldn't have other feelings about these troubling situations—it just means it's up to you to decide you won't drown in a victim mentality, not when there's still so much beauty in the world and in your life.

Practice empowered acceptance. If you turned down $30 in the experiment I mentioned before because your partner wanted to keep $70 for himself and then later you saw something you needed priced at $30, you'd likely

Continues

wish you had taken the offer. But you didn't because you were too caught up in your instinctive emotional response to rationally weigh the options. When you accept what is and then choose the best option for your future needs, that's empowered acceptance. Instead of bemoaning what you didn't get, you shift your focus to what you can do with what you got.

LOVE

WHY ARE
RELATIONSHIPS HARD?

~~~~~~~~~~~~~~~~~~~~~~~~~~~

If the shortest distance between two points is a straight line, then relationships may be the straight line to happiness—at least that's what a lot of us think. There's abundant research showing meaningful social connections form one of the cornerstones of lasting joy; other studies suggest people with romantic partners experience a greater sense of well-being because commitment creates security. But oftentimes, we form unrealistic expectations of our romantic relationships, setting ourselves up for disappointment and conflict. In the early stage of love, we feel such a euphoric sense of bliss that it seems unlikely our peace will ever fade—but everything morphs over time. No feeling is permanent.

At first in a new relationship, we feel a dramatic shift in our happiness, bathed as we are in the excitement and novelty of someone's adoration and attention. Eventually we accept this new situation as the norm, what psychologists refer to as *hedonic adaptation,* and go back to our original happiness set point—the general level of contentment we inevitably return to regardless of what good or bad things happen to us.

Though recent studies reveal that our set points can shift over time, other people can't be solely responsible for those changes. No one person can dramatically and permanently alter how we feel on the whole. Still, it's a lot safer to blame someone else for your dissatisfaction than to acknowledge they simply masked it for a while. True to the definition of insanity—doing the same things over and over again and expecting different results—we try to shape other people into what we think they need to be to re-create our initial happiness. Or as the play title suggests, we repeatedly say, "I love you. You're perfect. Now change."

It's not just with romantic relationships that we expect too much of people. We look to our friends and family to validate how we see the world, yet we get frustrated when they reflect things back at us that we'd rather not believe about ourselves. We look to other people to complete us, yet we feel stifled when we realize being completed by someone else is a choice to not be free. We expect people to act in our best interests, and yet in focusing on those needs, we sometimes fail to give that same selflessness in return. Relationships can get messy because they aren't just about two people existing in the same space together. They're about two people who want things from each other, when oftentimes what we really want is to get those things for ourselves.

For as long as I can remember, I assumed the answer to my happiness had something to do with other people. It was a safe conclusion when you consider my debilitating fear of everyone who wasn't me. If other people were the reason I was unhappy as well as the answer to finding greater happiness, I didn't actually have to do anything. I could just sit around counting the ways I'd been wronged, fantasizing about a type of love that would melt all memories of a painful past.

It's a tricky dichotomy, fearing people but wanting to be close to them. How can you create the possibility of love and acceptance if you block all attempts at emotional intimacy? For me, it revolved around Internet dating—the only way to fully vet a potential mate without having to meet him, open up to him, or risk disappointment or rejection. It's like people-watching on the web, as remorse-free as window shopping or getting a virtual makeover.

I thought if I just saw enough pictures and read enough descriptions, I'd find what I was looking for—a soul mate, my other half—and then I wouldn't feel so empty and lonely. I knew that people always said you meet someone when you're not looking, but I wasn't willing to risk not finding. I thought the only way to complete myself was to get proactive and find the man who would do it for me. I was prepared to spend countless hours dreaming, searching, wanting, hoping, and bemoaning my single life if it meant someone else would see the good in me and give me permission to stop focusing on the bad.

In my first year in San Francisco, I decided that love was a numbers game, like telemarketing and banner ads. I went on seventeen dates from *Craigslist*, fifteen from *eHarmony*, and twenty-six from *Match.com*. It wasn't until my sole *MySpace* dating experience that I decided to reevaluate my quest for love.

Dan (name changed) lived nearby and, according to his profile, enjoyed movies, sushi, and laughing. I *also* enjoy movies, sushi, and laughing, so I thought we were off to a promising start. Dan was the CEO of a solar energy company—a check on my list next to "making a difference in the world." He was tall with boyish good looks and a talent for active listening. On our first date, he nodded his head, appeared to deeply contemplate what I believed to be profound thoughts, and asked questions as if my stories intrigued him. He was less forthcoming in sharing information about himself, but his reserved aloofness was kind of charming. Perhaps it was my way of sabotaging the now to avoid hurt later, but I used to put everything out there way too soon on dates. Dan couldn't have been more different.

We had four coy, me-dominated dinner conversations before Dan told me, in the same stoic way he said everything else, that he had herpes. He may as well have been asking me to pass the salt; he was just that nonchalant. I wasn't entirely shocked. I left most dates with massive bombshells to weigh, like something out of a bad movie montage. There was the man who told me he was a priest, but he and God had an open relationship. There was the guy who wanted to lick my feet, and not just at some point, but right then, under the table. And let's not forgot the sex victim-cum-offender. (I couldn't if I tried.) I was so conditioned to expect red flags that I actually felt grateful when they were merely your garden-variety warning signs, like tales of womanizing and bachelor tendencies. As someone who frequently searched online for love, while secretly fearing I didn't deserve love, I understood that dating on the web entailed a lot of baggage sorting. And for a long time, I felt comfortable doing it. I thought I was less likely to be judged and hurt by men who'd probably felt those things many times before.

I could feel in my bones how painful it must have been to disclose his disease, knowing full well that many women would recoil in anger and possibly repulsion. Though I somewhat hesitated to set a precedent for physical closeness, my inner Florence Nightingale took over, tossing my arms around him. He said I was the first woman who didn't yell at him, hit him, or otherwise imply that he was somehow dirty or damaged. Since I hadn't put myself at risk, I felt worse for him than I did for me. I had an imploded fantasy of a future with a handsome, successful man who let me ramble about myself, but he had an incurable disease and an uphill battle if he was determined to date within the STD-free population.

Though our relationship was clearly limited, I told him to pick me up the following Friday at seven. Since I knew we'd have tons of time to simply talk, without the usual pressure to get physical, I felt open to developing this unconventional relationship. Underneath that justification was an even sadder belief: I wasn't sure I could attract a man who could give me everything I wanted. After all, I was part of the Internet dating crowd—not a dabbler, but a card-carrying member—and I came with an overflowing baggage cart. At least he would support me emotionally, I thought. And he'd be too grateful for my support to hurt me.

Over the next month, we fell into a routine of hanging out and watching movies, like an old married couple after the romance has long since gone. Our differences were like night and day. I have the kind of energy that manifests in rambling and leg twitching; he's about as lively as a houseplant with a poker face à la Stanley from *The Office*. I'm a creative type who believes in following my bliss; he's an entrepreneur who, as I slowly learned, believes money heals all wounds. I have a bleeding heart that constantly drips down my sleeve; he's about as emotional as a mainframe. I wondered what it felt like not to feel—to think of everything rationally, see everything in dollars and cents instead of bouncing from emotion to emotion. I imagined he was probably a lot happier, and yet I still wanted to change him. An apathetic joy couldn't possibly be right—not in general, and definitely not for me.

Three months into our G-rated dating, I started talking about wanting to do something meaningful online through my first blog, *Seeing Good*, which would be about expecting and seeing the best things in life instead of fearing and finding the worst. I was just starting to understand how profoundly an attitude adjustment can change the world I experience. My idea was to create a blog about positive thinking that would give 50 percent of the ad revenue back to the readers through a monthly drawing. I thought it would be a wonderful way to spread a positive message while doing a positive thing for subscribers. I could earn just enough, and give the rest away. That was something I could feel good about.

When I told Dan my idea, while he was searching through pay channels for yet another movie, he shared his feelings in a way he had never done before. "It won't work," he said. "You might feel all warm and fuzzy when you write it, but no one will care enough to come back and create substantial revenue. People just aren't as good and caring as you think they are. Most people are selfish—and you're no different."

That's when I recoiled—honestly, in anger and repulsion. How could he possibly think that way about people, and about *me*? What hope is there in life if you don't eventually find a light in yourself and recognize that same light in other people? Maybe he was just trying to hurt me. Maybe he was frustrated by our platonic closeness. Maybe he sensed that I was using him to fill a void in myself. Or maybe Occam's razor was ringing true again: maybe he said those things because he meant them. He had a right to, just as I had a right not to.

We could both see things completely differently without either of us being wrong. It just meant we were wrong for each other. I'd known for a while that our relationship, pseudo romance, friendship, whatever, would have a limited shelf life, and yet I dragged it out anyway. It was easier to stick with something that probably wouldn't be fulfilling, trying to smash a square peg into a round hole, than to let go and risk not finding something better. A bad romance felt better than none at all.

That's when I formed three conclusions that forever changed how I viewed relationships: First, I would never attract the right person if I wasn't willing to become the woman he deserved. Second, if I wanted to feel complete in a relationship, I had to complete myself first. And third, if I wanted to be in a relationship that was right, I had to be in it for the right reasons.

Though I have been in a mutually satisfying relationship for the last two years, I am by no means an expert—and maintaining the satisfaction is by no means easy. So long as we can see other people and feel, we will be tempted to create connections between the two, sometimes with good reason, and other times without. We will expect things, want things, try to change things, try to force things, say harsh things, and inevitably regret things. We'll pull close sometimes and push away at others. We'll feel suspicious at times and trusting at others.

It's impossible to be part of a relationship that is completely without friction, and to some extent, that's healthy, if we've chosen to be with people who are good for us. If we handle conflict well, we can challenge each other, strengthen each other, and grow closer to each other. In understanding what creates those conflicts, we can best plan to deal with them well. With that in mind I asked on Twitter, "Why are relationships hard?"

Relationships are mirrors

Relationships are reflections of how we see ourselves. Getting to know yourself is not easy. ~@Matt_Arguello

Relationships show us our shadow. For most of us, it's painful to see and be with. ~@lisadelrio

Relationships are hard because they never live up to our unrealistic ideals, and because they expose our insecurities. ~@amanofpeace

In relationships, you come face to face with yourself. ~@chancebuddhism

Relationships can be hard because they mirror the unresolved within, and confront parts of you which you could otherwise avoid resolving. ~@Falcongriffith

Everything you see outside yourself is a reflection of what's going on inside. When you're angry, you notice insensitive, rude people. When you're rushed, life seems to move at a glacial pace just to get in your way. Relationships are just more persistently uncomfortable because the mirror moves.

In his book *Free to Love, Free to Heal*, Deepak Chopra outlines seven principles that help us feel love more freely, the first addressing this very idea. He explains that when there is dissonance in a relationship, it serves us best to look inside ourselves and question what we can do to address it. If we're looking for more attention and appreciation, perhaps we could be more attentive and appreciative. That's not to say we shouldn't communicate what we want and need. It's just that oftentimes we get frustrated trying to change other people when it's far more empowering to make a change within ourselves—and as a natural consequence, to manifest change in the world around us.

Mirroring isn't just about being the change we want to see. Sometimes we see in other people what we hold within our own hearts but would prefer to deny. It's not always easy to acknowledge our weaknesses, but that doesn't mean we're not aware subconsciously, and that doesn't mean we won't eventually recognize them. Sometimes it's easier to notice them in someone else—whether they're actually there or not. Psychologists talk about *projecting*, the act of denying our own traits and then ascribing them to another person. It's a defense mechanism that allows us to avoid accepting qualities or thoughts we'd rather not have. Sigmund Freud explained that projection helps us minimize guilt since it allows us to avoid owning an undesirable trait.

People project onto each other all the time. A competitive friend of mine once asked me if I suspected everyone who knew me wanted me to fail in life—that other people were jealous and felt threatened by any successes I had. Knowing her as well as I did, I couldn't help but wonder if this was an unintentional confession that she actually felt that way. I was equally guilty. The second she said it I projected selfishness onto her, when that was really my biggest fear about myself.

Getting mindful about mirroring and projection is one of the healthiest things we can do for our relationships, but our egos aren't always thrilled about our challenging of ourselves. If our thoughts, beliefs, and feelings make up our identities, any insinuation that they should change immediately feels threatening. How can you consider changing what you think if you believe that you are your thoughts? Changing them would be like death. How can you acknowledge your weaknesses if you suspect they have to define you? Recognizing them would be tantamount to labeling yourself damaged.

Or maybe not. Maybe being honest with ourselves and taking responsibility for our feelings toward other people can be ultimately empowering. When you consider that what you see in other people lives somewhere in you, you also open yourself up to the possibility of noticing beauty you never knew you had. In yoga, we always end class with the Sanskrit word *namaste*, which means, "The light in me honors the light in you." Just like we can see the less appealing parts of ourselves in other people, we can identify the good as well.

Everything we see in others, we have within ourselves some-where. If you envy someone who is brave, know that you have the ability to be brave, too. If you're fascinated by some-one who is selfless, know that you have that same selflessness locked inside you. We are all made of the same stuff, and we all have the same potential to make both mistakes and mir-acles. The only differences between us revolve around where we focus our attention and what we choose to do.

That being said, it's admittedly a lot easier to own a posi-tive trait than it is a negative one. It's why parents frequently take credit for the good things their kids do and assume the bad comes from their spouse's side of the family. No one wants to identify with a negative behavior—in turn, we end up judging other people's actions out of fear of acknowl-edging we are just like them. When we reject someone else, refusing to muster compassion, what we're really doing is responding to them in the way we'd respond to ourselves: harshly and shamefully.

My current relationship is the first long-term one I've been in since college, meaning I casually dated for nearly a decade. Ehren is kind, selfless, likeable, carefree, and wise beyond his years. It seems to me that it isn't a coincidence I am suddenly in a healthy relationship with an admirable person after I chose to start actively being the person I want to be. I simply couldn't see good in someone else or be good for him until I felt good about who I was. I couldn't learn to give someone the benefit of the doubt instead of suspecting he meant to hurt me until I stopped believing I deserved to hurt. There is a direct correlation between what we feel and what we see, and the two are always in flux. When you realize that everyone has darkness and light, and accept yourself for both, you're better equipped to embrace other people as they are, without the weight of your guilt or fears. More simply put: only when you're able to be kind and loving to yourself can you give and receive the same to and from someone else.

Create a better relationship reflection.

If you find yourself feeling angry and judgmental toward someone you love:

Before you judge, ask yourself if you hold the quality that you're judging. Maybe you suspect your boyfriend of cheating because you're a flirty person and you assume he's doing the same. Or perhaps you think your wife's lazy, and it really bothers you because your father always called you lazy. Recognize that you hold that quality, and how you feel when you acknowledge that you do. Odds are the anger isn't coming from what the other person did or may do—it's how you feel about owning that trait.

Continues

Address the feelings beneath what you're projecting. If you're projecting something you feel guilty about, either fess up or change your choices so that you don't continue to feel so conflicted and suspicious. If you're projecting something that you don't like about yourself, offer yourself a little compassion and forgiveness so that you'll be able to offer the same to someone else who embodies that trait. So long as you feel shame over a quality, you will recognize and vehemently oppose it in others. The only way to accept other people and give them the love they deserve is to first accept and love yourself.

Ask yourself every day how you can create the image you'd like to reflect. If you want a significant other who is independent, caring, considerate, and brave, decide to nurture those qualities in yourself every day. Make self-care a priority. Consistently reach out to the people you love to let them know you're there for them. Most likely they will reciprocate—and with much more joy and less resentment than if you badgered them. And if they don't return this same love-in-action, because you're proud of who you are, you'll likely feel healthy and strong enough to walk away, open and receptive to better matches.

We have to complete ourselves without attaching to someone else for happiness

Relationships are hard because we often seek from others what we are not giving ourselves. ~**@arvinddevalia**

It is easy to forget that you must continue to love yourself. ~**@anibunny**

Sometimes we expect others to fill the emptiness that only we can fill ourselves. ~@**nhweas**

Relationships are hard because we worry about what we can get from them instead of what we can give. ~@**unjordi**

It is hard to have but not to hold too tightly—to enjoy closeness without the trap of attachment to the closeness. ~@**SevenZark**

When Jerry Maguire said, "You complete me," he set romantic hearts aflutter around the world, perpetuating an unhealthy idea that we can somehow fill voids within each other. Tom Cruise can't take total credit for creating this codependent fantasy. The Greek philosopher Plato explored the idea in *The Symposium* between 385 and 380 BCE, suggesting the primal humans had both male and female parts but Zeus split them into two separate bodies. From that point on, the two halves were destined to search for each other— their "split apart" or soul mate—to become whole again.

The belief that somewhere in the world there is one perfect match for each of us feels much more special than the suggestion that we could be with any number of compatible people, if we choose to nurture long-term relationships. We don't want to think of finding love like choosing a job—discovering something that feels right and then doing the work. We want to think of love as something fated to make life require less work. We want to think of it as something profound, otherworldly, divine, even. We want our attraction to feel deeply spiritual, not rational or biological, so the comfort of codependence will seem less taboo and more enlightened.

Incomplete people can't possibly create a balanced relationship because they will always need to lean on each other. A friend of mine once suggested that people are like glasses of water. We have to come to each other already full or else one person will have to empty some of her glass into the other to even things out—but then you're both lacking, constantly filling each other to make up for your combined deficiencies. As someone who walked around one-fourth full for most of my life, desperately seeking three-fourths of my happiness, I can personally attest that it's nearly impossible to be satisfied in a relationship if you aren't already satisfied outside of it.

An old friend of mine I'll call Jade labeled herself a "consummate relationship girl." She was the polar opposite of my serial-dating twenties self. She was always coupled in a committed situation, and she rarely ended one without having the next lined up. If I would have asked Jade to describe herself, she'd have rattled off a list of labels that all revolved around being with someone else: nurturing, supportive, loving, dependable. It's almost as if she didn't exist unless she was in relation to another person. That's not to say the labels we put on ourselves necessarily have to define us. It's just that what we experience is a consequence of where we focus our attention. If we never cultivate our independent self, we won't have a lot to offer another person, other than selflessness with expectations of reciprocity.

That's what happened every time with Jade. She had a very clear idea of what another person should provide her, emotionally, physically, and spiritually. She gave all of herself, sacrificed indiscriminately, planned for the future after only a few dates, and eventually found herself feeling empty when that person didn't fulfill her needs. Sometimes he wanted to, but simply couldn't—like when her long-term boyfriend died in his early thirties. It would have been tragic for anyone who loved him, regardless of level of attachment. But it was different for Jade. She didn't lose a part of herself in the figurative way, as we all do when someone we love disappears from our lives. She said that her life meant nothing after his death, and she didn't think she could live without him—which all changed a month later when she entered her next long-term relationship. Her earlier words were telling: her life had no meaning unless she was part of a couple.

The irony in defining ourselves through other people is that we're more apt to experience happiness in relationships if we're true to ourselves—which means we have to have a strong idea of who we are autonomously. There is nothing as liberating as authenticity, which is why we get comfortable in environments, jobs, and roles. The freedom to be unabashedly genuine provides much more peace than the suspicion we have to pretend we're something we're not. If you define yourself through an attachment to someone else, it's not always easy to know where you stop and he begins. How can you be true to your beliefs if you're willing to shape-shift to ensure you don't split apart again?

People often talk about getting married as if it's the answer to lasting happiness, and yet we all know countless married couples who have grown bitter and distant through the years. Our expectations set us up for disappointment because a bond with someone else can never fill the cracks in our own happiness. As Harvard psychology professor Daniel Gilbert said at the 2010 American Psychological Association convention, "It's not marriage that makes you happy. It's happy marriage that makes you happy." Happy people are more apt to create happy marriages.

And whole people are more apt to feel whole in relationships. So the real question here is: what does it mean—and what does it take—to feel whole?

Stay whole in and out
of relationships.

If you feel like you need to be in a relationship to be complete:

Choose to do what you want to do today, whether you're single or in a relationship. If you're single, establish all the things that you've been waiting to do with a partner and then do them now—go on that vacation or enroll in that cooking class. Strive to become the kind of person who would complement, not complete, your future significant other. If you're in a relationship, make it a priority to do a little something you enjoy without your partner every day, whether it's taking a morning walk or going to lunch with friends. The goal is for your relationship to be part of your life, not all of it.

Practice daily self-love. And I'm referring to your authentic self—not just the self that most people see every day. Take time to write in a journal, or write music, or do whatever you can to acknowledge your feelings and accept and love yourself just as you are—light and dark. All too often, we depend on other people to make us feel okay about the less flattering parts of our personalities. Give yourself the validation you're hoping to get from someone else. Love yourself because of, not in spite of, your flaws.

Take the halo off your partner. If you feel like this is your one chance at love—that your significant other is your ultimate destiny—you will put a ton of pressure on the relationship, and also keep yourself feeling a sense of cosmic codependence. Remember that you have lots of relationships, and even if this one is special, there are lots of other special ones with friends and family members that you need to nurture. You may be great and happy in this relationship, but if it ended, you could also be great and happy outside of it.

Expectations put pressure on relationships

Relationships are hard because we expect them to be easy.
~@kolormyworld06

Relationships are hard because we put so much pressure not just on the relationship but the person we are with. ~@Ms_CRivera

When we bury our loved ones under the burden of our expectations, at that time our relationship stops breathing. ~@kumudinni

We think our partner should be perfect but give ourselves a lot of room for error. ~@karawow

We always try to change the other party according to our own idea about them. ~@mayasaputra

Positive people expect the best, as opposed to their negative counterparts, who expect the worst so they'll be pleasantly surprised if something good happens. Neither of these attitudes leads to healthy relationships. In his August 26, 2010, post on *PsychologyToday.com*, Mark D. White referred to expectations as the other side of obligations, and suggested that both of them signal problems in a relationship. If we communicate our needs well, we should *want* to meet each other's out of love and appreciation, not obligation, and we shouldn't necessarily form expectations of what that love and appreciation will look like because that isn't very loving or appreciative.

White ended his post by saying this may be a naïve and overly romantic simplification; perhaps it is, but there's something to this idea. Most of the time, when there's conflict in a relationship, it's because one person didn't meet the other's expectations. From the moment when we first meet someone else, we start forming them, if not consciously, subconsciously.

First there's the idealism expectation: we'll somehow complete each other. Since it just isn't possible to give someone else what he hasn't given himself, this is our choice to eventually feel disillusioned with love. Then there are past-driven expectations: our relationships will look like the best that's come and gone and nothing like the worst. Every new relationship is different, and a new partner can't possibly be responsible for what happened before. A new boyfriend shouldn't have to pay for an old one's infidelity; a new girlfriend shouldn't have to like PDA because an old one would make out everywhere from traffic court to the dentist's office. After that, there's the infinite-euphoria expectation: the honeymoon-phase high will last, and if it doesn't, something must be wrong. It isn't— in fact, it's more likely something is wrong if you never feel comfortable enough around each other for your relationship to seem at least somewhat unexciting.

This is just the tip of the expectation iceberg, but the rest of it offers more of the same: expecting our significant others to cause us pleasure and not pain—even if we are actually responsible for feeling pain because of the way we translate what happens. If you always sacrifice for your husband and he doesn't do the same for you, you may assume he doesn't care enough to put in the same effort. But maybe his behavior doesn't mean that at all; it could just mean he didn't realize you were overextending yourself to get something specific in return. If you have a passion that you wish your girlfriend shared, you may feel bitter whenever she doesn't join you, assuming she doesn't care about your interests. But maybe it only means she respects herself enough to honor what's right for her and assumes you would do the same.

The most damaging expectation of all is that other people are somehow responsible for our feelings. For the longest time, I was caught in a vicious cycle: I ignored my own needs until I exploded on some undeserving person, blaming him for all the emotions I had stuffed down for weeks prior. I'd ignore what I wanted to please other people, put their needs above my own to make them like me, fail to set boundaries, and generally expect that other people would make sure our relationships were worth my effort. After a couple weeks of martyrdom, I would feel frustration, anger, resentment, disappointment, and sadness bubble up inside me, but I'd have no idea what caused them. It would be like a tidal wave of emotion, with blotchy eyes, heaving sobs, and chest convulsions.

It was far easier to point fingers at everyone around me than it was to consider I'd caused this tsunami of angst. It was my friend's fault I was so upset—she only called me when she needed something and never really cared how I was doing. It wasn't that I chose to overextend myself in helping her and rarely asked her for what I needed. Or it was my boyfriend's fault that I was upset—he didn't work as hard as I did, which put a lot of pressure on me. It wasn't that I chose to say yes to every request and overwhelmed my schedule. If someone else was responsible for my emotion overload, it was no longer my sole burden to carry. What I didn't consider is that when we burden someone else, we take away our power to change our own feelings, and we also compromise a relationship that could help evoke positive ones.

Now when I'm feeling something uncomfortable that I can't identify, I look for reasons rooted in my own choices. Sometimes I still need things from my family and friends, but the responsibility for changing my feelings starts with me and what I choose to say and do. The same is true for all of us.

This doesn't mean we shouldn't have *any* expectations of people. In her book *5 Simple Steps to Take Your Marriage from Good to Great*, Terri Orbuch highlights the difference between realistic and unrealistic expectations. While it's unrealistic to suggest that, if you love each other, your passion will never fade, it *is* realistic to expect that, if you take time to communicate with each other, you can prevent unnecessary drama later. It's also realistic to expect that if someone loves you, she is generally doing the best she can; if you need more than what you're getting, so long as it's not unreasonable, she will make every effort to give it. Of course, that also starts with you—whether or not you choose to acknowledge what you need, express it clearly, and then give back out of love, not obligation.

Communicate needs and reduce expectations.

If you feel like your expectations aren't being met:

Ask for what you need and expect nothing more. This doesn't mean your loved ones won't do things for you without you needing to ask for them specifically—it just means they will know to do the things that are important, and the rest will be icing on the cake. If you enjoy getting flowers at work, ask your boyfriend if he'd surprise you with them sometime in the next month because it really makes your day. If you want your girlfriend to spend more time with your family, tell her it's important to you and see

Continues

how she feels about it. You can reasonably expect only what you're willing to ask for.

Do what you need to do for you. Everyone has personal needs, whether it's going to the gym after work or taking some alone time on Saturday morning. If someone asks you to do something and your instinct is to honor your own need, do that. Anything you would expect a partner to do for you—love you, understand you, take care of you: make sure that you are actively doing those things for yourself every day. If you don't take care of yourself, you will likely form even stronger expectations of your partner because there will be such a large void to fill.

Create an environment of thoughtfulness. Oftentimes when relationships grow, the little things fall to the wayside. Both sides resent that, and neither makes the proactive choice to re-create that same thoughtfulness. Set the tone for the relationship you want. If you expect small gestures of love and support, make a point to start offering them. You're not giving to be able to then expect these same things in return—rather, you're taking responsibility for being in the kind of relationship where these things come more naturally to both of you.

Relationships are hard because we fight for our perceptions

Relationships involve people and people are universes. Can you imagine universes colliding? ~@uno_br

Everyone is a little nuts in their own way and few people acknowledge this. Recognize the mixed nuts of humans. ~@TangoKarnitz

Relationships are hard because each person's perception is uniquely theirs, and they react from this place of perception. ~@SuliloByDebbie

Relationships require conscious effort and a diminished ego, both difficult in autonomous individualistic societies. ~@spitzmpa

Relationships are hard because they mean so much. Two people can't always be on the same page. Our uniqueness is beautiful and challenging. ~@NikkiFaith

Most of us guard our perceptions of the world for dear life. In his book *Making Up the Mind: How the Brain Creates Our Mental World*, Chris Frith, a professor of cognitive neurology, explains that how we see the world is largely a product of interpretations based on memories of the past. Since we all have different backgrounds, none of us sees things exactly the same as another person does, and we tend to associate ourselves with the understandings we've developed—as if those perceptions make up our identities. When the future unfolds as we expected based on the ideas we formed, we feel a sense of security; when the outside world fails to corroborate what we think we know, we feel threatened. It's almost as if we don't know who we are when the external world doesn't authenticate us.

That's why most of us align ourselves with friends who see things the same way we do; these are the people who "get" us. This isn't as relevant for our *weak ties*—the term sociologists use to define our acquaintances, colleagues, and other loose connections. But in our strong, intimate relationships, we expect that other people will consistently confirm our views and, in doing so, validate us. When they don't seem to get us, or don't act in accordance with our ideas of how things should work, that's when trouble starts—and usually we assume we're right and someone else is wrong.

It's also why we often believe we were right even after it's clear we weren't. Psychologists refer to this as *hindsight bias*—when we assume we knew something before we learned it or could have predicted something before it happened, even though we didn't. David McRaney, who authors a blog called *You Are Not So Smart: A Celebration of Self-Delusion*, wrote an interesting post about this idea in which he cited two research studies about older people. One revealed that they don't accept new information well, just like an old dog can't learn new tricks, and the other suggested that elderly people, equipped with years of wisdom, tend to complete college degrees more quickly than young people who have brains that aren't completely formed. Then McRaney dropped the bombshell: he actually made both of those studies up, and yet they both appeared to offer common-sense conclusions that we might assume we already knew. We generally revise our past beliefs to feel secure in the knowledge we were, at least on some level, right.

Back in college, I had a friend who had to be right about everything and was willing to create excruciating drama with friends and relatives to ensure they agreed with her. Let's call her Jessica. It started with little absolutes, like putting the toilet paper on a certain way or taking a specific route on the road, and extended into major things, like religion and politics. Being around Jessica was exhausting because I never knew when she'd cross-examine me to find cracks in my beliefs. I understood her insecurity because I felt equally threatened when other people didn't agree with me; I was just passive-aggressive in my coercion because I was desperate to get other people's approval.

We had a major falling out at the end of our freshman year because I decided to re-audition for the acting program after originally being rejected. She had already auditioned a second time and failed to make the cut. After that, she decided no one should bother re-auditioning because it was impossible to get in if you didn't before your freshman year. She spent two weeks trying to convince me not to try—first overtly and then subtly when I made it clear I wasn't giving up. I guessed that it would be difficult on her ego to challenge that belief she'd formed, but I wasn't willing to just accept her conclusion without finding out for myself. When I got accepted into the program, she altered her deduction. It was no longer true that *no one* could become an acting major as a sophomore; it was just that she was Spanish and the head of the program was a racist—which she said she'd suspected all along.

On some level, we all get attached to our ideas—ideas about what's good and what's bad, ideas about how other people should act, and ideas about how people should respond to us. When other people don't fall in line, we think ourselves into anxiety. We know what beliefs feel safe, and we'd often rather be miserable than risk compromising them. We'd rather fight the people we love, forcing them to deal with the discomfort of admitting they are wrong than consider that maybe *no one* is wrong—we just see things differently. Or maybe we *are*, in fact, wrong, and if we consider that possibility, we can gain new knowledge and actually be right in the future.

If we can accept that we are not our perceptions, and if we look objectively at our stress when we feel the need to fight for them, our relationships can be far more peaceful. It won't always be easy—it's instinctive to respond to the world based on what we've learned before and what makes us feel secure. A good way to challenge this impulse is to question: what's more important—being right or being happy? If you value the person you're inclined to fight and it doesn't hurt you or your relationship to avoid an argument that your ego wants to have, agree to disagree and move on. Letting go of an idea doesn't have to deconstruct you if it allows you to better understand and accept someone you love. And in the end, that's what keeps our relationships alive and well: a commitment to understanding and loving each other more often than we fear and fight each other.

Choose being happy over being right.

If you find yourself fighting over beliefs or ideas:

Choose your battles. On the one hand, you have to tell people when there's something bothering you. That's the only way to address problems. On the other hand, you don't have to let everything bother you. If you're not sure if this is something worth bringing up, ask yourself: *Does this happen often and leave me feeling bad? Will this really matter in the grand scheme of things? Can I empathize with their feelings instead of dwelling on my insecurity?*

Get to the root of the situation. On the surface, you might be fighting over money, but there may be other feelings underneath the actual issue—in fact, there may even be residual feelings from another event fueling this conversation. Stop and ask yourself and the other person: what's the real issue here?

Continues

Challenge the urge to lay out your evidence. We all become armchair lawyers when it comes to defending what we believe is right—and sometimes that means we are formulating our evidence instead of really listening to what someone else is saying. Decide that you won't interrupt and that instead you'll listen with an open mind. You can hear someone out without having to adopt her beliefs. Simply hear them out. Decide that it's more important to be in a relationship where both people feel heard and respected than in a relationship where both constantly fight to be right.

Get comfortable saying, "Let's agree to disagree." People with different backgrounds will naturally see things differently sometimes. Neither of you need to be wrong. This is a choice to maintain what feels right for you without having to invalidate what feels right for someone you love. If it's something that you need to form some type of consensus on—like how to raise your children or what to do with an inheritance—focus on meeting in the middle. It's not about one of you getting what you want; it's about finding a mutually agreeable solution. It's about loving and respecting each other enough that you want to meet halfway. And if you don't legitimately want that, then it's about letting go and opening up to the right relationship—one where happiness together will feel more important than self-righteousness alone.

MONEY

DO YOU NEED MONEY TO BE HAPPY?

In the documentary Lucky that I mentioned before, which chronicles the lives of several lottery winners, the two people who suggested they were destined to win $110 million offered an interesting insight into the effects of money on relationships. After they won, many of their closest friends could no longer relate to them. Caught up in the pressure of his own financial struggles, one of them even commented that he felt sick to his stomach just looking at his newly wealthy friends. Perhaps this goes back to that research on our collective fixation with fairness; a lottery winner didn't actually have to work for that money and yet, in the blink of an eye, her life became instantly easier—at least from most people's perspectives.

Of course that suspicion isn't consistent with the research on lottery winners, which paints a picture of listlessness, depression, alcoholism, incarceration, and even suicide. A massive windfall inevitably incites envy, putting a strain on relationships. If it's public, it also makes you a target for criminals who see opportunity in your fortune. And then there's the question of how to spend the money and fill the time in which you don't need to work to make a living. People often assume that not having to do anything is the surest path to bliss. But the reality is that time is the ultimate asset, and we're more likely to experience happiness if we spend it in a way that fulfills us, whether we need the money it generates or not.

In the beginning of 2008, I was working a temp job in San Francisco. Prior to that, I'd worked for over a hundred other employers, if you counted all my full-time positions and short-term supplemental gigs. I'd worn a lot of different hats but they were all too big, too small, or too itchy. I'd also never earned more than $30,000 annually, even though I certainly worked hard—yet I always believed I could eventually amass great wealth if I just kept pushing myself (an expectation I share with the majority of other US citizens who believe in the American Dream—a whopping 72 percent even after the economic meltdown, according to a 2009 CBS News poll). Though I've never been much for things, like most of us, I often indulged the fantasy of a life with a lot more freedom. If only I could work hard enough to eventually work less, then everything would be perfect—in that magical tomorrow when there are fewer obstacles and more reasons to bust out the good champagne.

One Monday in February, I secured two jobs. That morning, a start-up company in Menlo Park offered me a position earning more than $50,000 annually before bonuses. As the site's content manager, I would write their blog posts, sales copy, and weekly newsletters. Later that night, partially drunk from celebrating, I completed a phone interview for a twenty-hour-per-week writing position with a pet website and somehow got the job. I was guilty of IUI—interviewing under the influence—and yet it worked in my favor. I'd sent my resume to nearly one hundred companies before getting those two calls, and in less than twenty-four hours I got a massive return on my time investment.

I told both employers I was available to start the following Monday, giving myself a running start to rearrange my life for this seventy-plus-hour weekly schedule, which would earn me more than $75,000 annually. The first thing I did was buy a car, a used one I found on Craigslist. I then found an apartment in San Mateo, twenty-five miles south of San Francisco and twenty-five miles north of Menlo Park. It was my first apartment on my own, and it came with access to a gym, a pool, and a pond with a fountain. My rent more than doubled, but it appeared to be worth it. I imagined myself walking into my own home, hanging my key on a kitschy key holder right near the door, and then standing regally on the balcony with a glass of wine, like a bona fide hardworking, respectable adult. I was willing to spend a lot of hours to buy that one minute of pride.

In the first few weeks of my new full-time job, I worked from nine to seven and stayed up until midnight completing my pet-related writing. Knowing the overtime at my full-time job would end in a month, when I went from contractor to official employee, I maintained this schedule for the next three weeks, rarely even seeing those fun amenities I'd bought into. I did very little other than work, but I was paying down my credit cards and building up my savings account. Since all the friends I'd made in San Francisco were now a half-hour away, I had very little distracting me from money making. Each month when I put $1,000 in the bank, I felt smart, capable, valuable, in control, and well on my way to something better.

I didn't have time for a life outside the buildings where I lived and worked, except for yoga between jobs, but this seemed fine to me—that is, until those buildings became one and the same. In August, my company's Israeli headquarters decided to shut down the US office. Most of my colleagues were expendable because they had counterparts in Tel Aviv, but at the time, I was the only writer on the team. When they offered to keep me on as a work-from-home employee, it seemed like I'd hit the jackpot. I could set my own schedule, turn my balcony into my office, work in my pajamas, *and* shave an hour of drive time off my day—and let's not forget the occasional lunchtime margarita I could now have whenever I wanted.

It took me roughly two weeks to feel trapped by my situation. I didn't work on my balcony that first day because I never took a shower, and my hair stuck up like something out of my junior high yearbook, just a couple years after the '80s. Even if I *had* showered, there was also the issue of my furniture deficiency; I only had a houseplant outside those sliding glass doors, and I also lacked a kitchen table or desk inside, making my couch my official workspace. I never had a lunchtime margarita because my workload increased now that I was the only remaining employee from my old team. Even without the hour commute, I added two hours to my workday, and still had freelance work to complete.

I rarely left my apartment. Sunday through Friday, I worked from sunup to sundown, and on Saturday I caught up on sleep. My long hours were partly due to the fact that we were using a new proprietary system for our hundred weekly newsletters, and the software team frequently deleted my work when they made tweaks within the code. Without the forced socialization of a workplace, I hardly ever interacted with actual human beings, except when the deliveryman brought my Chinese food. My couch became less and less firm over time—I actually had nightmares that it would morph into a microfiber version of *Little Shop of Horrors*'Audrey II and swallow me whole—yet I never considered buying appropriate furniture. Turning my apartment into a business suite made the whole work-from-home thing seem a lot less fun. Eventually I started changing out of my pajamas—but most days I just put on other pajamas, albeit clean ones that didn't smell like night sweat. I constantly felt overworked, overwhelmed, exhausted, and anxious about the potential to get to one in the morning without completing everything.

Yet I did the same thing, day after day, feeling unfulfilled, unhappy, unbalanced, and resistant to doing anything about it. I was writing, and I was making good money. What more could I possibly want? What more was there? If I didn't keep doing what I was doing, how could I possibly get ahead? What hope did I have to be successful if I wasn't willing to work harder than other people? If I left the sure thing I had, particularly when other people were losing their jobs, what would I do instead? I had to keep pushing. It's the only way to get to the other side.

One Friday night when I'd been awake for thirty-six hours with my laptop fused to my legs, I heard my neighbors laughing their way to the elevator. I imagined the streets they might cross, the private jokes they might tell, and the rounds they might buy for each other later. I seriously considered folding myself into their mob in the hopes they wouldn't realize I wasn't one of them. Just then an email popped up in my stream. One of the women who had been on my Steps Across America team had just published her first children's book—in between weeks when she traveled the world and wrote about it for a series of websites. I couldn't even get through the first paragraph without feeling a sucker punch of paralyzing envy. Here she was—someone who had once shared a journey with me, who had since used her time to do so many passionate, powerful, purposeful things. And all the friends she had! Her Facebook page narrated a life of fun and inclusion, a life she had chosen and created and was now nurturing.

For a minute I felt incredibly guilty for wanting to delete her email without even feeling a shred of happiness for her. Then all of a sudden, that guilt turned into gratitude. I didn't want to steal her happiness or success. I had no investment in her failure or dissatisfaction. I just wanted the courage to be more like her. I wanted to enjoy my hours. I wanted to feel a sense of meaning. I wanted to unplug unless being plugged in somehow aligned with my values and helped me make a difference in the world. Most of all, I wanted to know that when someone around me made a choice to live out loud, I would be able to rejoice in her happiness because I wasn't bitter about withholding it from myself.

Right then I decided I was not going to keep working that night—or any night. I'd spent too many years sitting alone, waiting to live, to now excuse that same isolation with a paycheck. We were not meant to fill our days with to-do lists, emails, and spreadsheets. No dream or goal is worth completely sacrificing today's hours in the hopes tomorrow's will somehow be better. There is no other side to get to. There is no ahead to rush toward. Even a sure thing can be a surefire path to misery if it isn't the thing we want to be doing.

I decided to quit my full-time job and maintain the pet website writing gig to get by, which would have been a pretty smart plan if they hadn't both laid me off the following week. Unlike in the past, when unemployment felt like freedom because no one was depending on me, unemployment now felt like freedom because *I* was depending on me. In my newly empty schedule I amped up my yoga practice and starting planning to turn the little daily-quote Twitter account I ran into a website about happiness, positivity, and wisdom. When I finally launched *TinyBuddha.com* after months of planning, I pulled out the good champagne—and by good champagne, I mean Brut. That year I made less than $30,000, and yet I had everything I needed to be happy.

This might seem like a logical point to end this conversation on money and happiness. If we enjoy our time, we don't need money, right? Unfortunately, that's not the case—money is a necessity. After my unemployment benefits ran out in the beginning of 2010, I faced a problem most of us can relate to: once we identify our passion, we then have to figure out how we can sustain ourselves doing it. What exactly is enough for sustenance? If we do what we love, will the money come, making that a moot point? If the money *does* come, will we enjoy our passion all the more because we don't have to worry about surviving? And when we think about all those factors—everything that complicates the simple decision to spend our time in a way that feels meaningful—it is worth asking again: do you need money to be happy? This was one of the last questions I asked on Twitter.

Money can help if you're already happy

You can use money to be happy, but if you rely on it to find happiness then it will end up using you. All is already provided. ~@gabrielive

You need consistency, security, and autonomy to truly be happy. Money contributes to all three, but so does passion. ~@strangerdaze

All one needs to be happy is to make the decision. Might as well decide to be happy with money rather than without money. ~@joyousexpansion

You don't need money to be happy. All you really need to do is to open your eyes to the beauty around you. ~@YouKnowJayCub

Money is an essential part to happiness. It gives us a stress-free life. But without loved ones, none of that money will mean anything. ~@KristenBaert

With all the statistics about miserable trust-fund babies and suicidal lottery winners, I couldn't help wondering if there are any people who've hit the jackpot and are blissfully happy. As much as we all might intellectually know the research on money and happiness, a lot of us still suspect our lives would be infinitely better if we suddenly had millions to play with. Maybe it's true for some people. Just because the media likes telling us stories of lottery winners who lost it, wished they never won it, or gave it all away, that doesn't mean that's universally the case. It just means the media knows what sells—controversial tales of gain, loss, and maybe even a compelling comeback.

In *Lucky*, Mike Pace, a former Powerball announcer, asked of lottery winners, "Do you become what you dreamed you would? Or do you become what you most deeply, secretly are?" That seems to be the million-dollar question—or the $25.4-million question, as those lottery totals usually somehow calculate out to. Can money actually change who you are, or does it merely magnify what lies under the surface?

Let's forget for a minute about massive wealth and think about even moderate good fortune. I've known quite a few people who have catapulted from lower middle class to upper middle class only to find themselves face-to-face with the reality of their unhappiness. Shortly after I graduated from college, when I accepted a $12 hourly job in social services, a friend of mine from the projects who didn't have a college degree started making more than $100K annually in sales. I'll call him Chrishere.

Chris got bullied a lot in school because he was quiet, his family was poor, and other people had a hard time understanding him. When he first started collecting those mammoth paychecks, earning more than many of his friends combined, it seemed like he had stumbled into the good life so many of us fantasize about. He walked with his head held high and looked people in the eye, as if he knew they respected him, or they should. He started talking more loudly than he did in high school, when he frequently mumbled, as if what he had to say might be unintelligent. He stopped complaining about his deadbeat dad who never so much as called let alone paid child support. Then he bought a car, a duplex, a whole new wardrobe—and, as I later learned, copious amounts of Vicodin and cocaine.

Having more money didn't change that, deep down, Chris felt embarrassed about where he came from. It also didn't change that he couldn't sleep at night without wondering why his father didn't seem to love him. Like many of us, he carried around a world of shame, regret, confusion, anger, and dissatisfaction, and mistakenly thought success would be the best revenge against everyone who had wronged him. It never occurred to him that revenge isn't the best reward—it's the best way to stay bitter. He didn't realize that money wasn't what he wanted—he wanted the feelings he assumed money could buy.

Money can't buy feelings. No amount of success can erase pain from the past. The only thing that allows us to fully appreciate and enjoy good fortune is a sense of peace with who we are, regardless of what we have or gain.

There have been many times in my life when I have channeled all my sadness into my checkbook. I had a magic number that made me feel in control—an arbitrary amount of money that I never wanted to spend but wanted to have sitting there like a thick, green security blanket. Since I have more often than not had less than that number, this gave me a focus for all of my frustrations. I wasn't unhappy because I was wasting the days away; it was because I didn't have that money. Life wasn't stressful because I made it that way; it was because I didn't have that money. That number was the answer to everything—until I got to that magic number, and then I decided to increase it.

That's how it is for a lot of us. We avoid acknowledging what's really bothering us and what we need to do to address that problem, and instead chase some random tomorrow that we hope will free us from our pain.

Just like with relationships, money can be the biggest possible disappointment if we've formed unrealistic expectations of what it can do. If you expect that money will melt away all your sadness, you will be disappointed. No amount of cash and coins can fill a hole in a heart. If you expect money will get you other people's approval, you will be disappointed. Affluence doesn't guarantee people will value who you are as a person. If you expect money will buy you other people's respect, you will be disappointed. People may be fascinated by wealth—and envious, because we assume it's a lucky shot with a happiness chaser—but none of us give automatic respect just because someone has amassed a fortune. Just like money, all those things have to be earned.

Money also can't change the fact that we all need to be responsible for creating happiness across all areas of our life. We need to be connected to other people, engaged in activities we enjoy, and committed to something that gives us meaning. We need to let go of anger and bitterness, forgive and love, accept and grow—all things that have no bearing on what we earn. It's possible to have all this and money, too, but without our intrinsic belief that life is valuable with or without riches, money is ultimately worthless.

Meet your future money expectations in the present.

If you've been hoping your whole life will change when you finally have more money:

Make a list of everything you think would change if you were wealthier. Think about all the feelings you generally try to escape by pushing yourself to be successful. Do you think you'd feel better about yourself? Would you feel more satisfied in life? Would you feel less worried? Less pressured? Less overwhelmed?

Now ask yourself: How can you create those feelings right now? If you think you'd feel better about yourself with more money, what actions can you take to operate with courage and integrity so that you feel good about the person you're being now? If you think you'd feel more satisfied, what would need to change in your professional life in order for you to feel more fulfilled and purposeful now? If you think you'd feel less worried, pressured, or overwhelmed, can you start meditating, so that worries have less of a hold on you now? You may very well have a lot more money someday, but if you answer these questions now, someday won't be the day you realize that money isn't enough.

Create a second list of everything that makes life valuable to you. This list might include spending time with your family, helping people, trying new things—whatever you treasure most in life. Now cross-reference this list with your schedule from the last week. Did you have sufficient time to incorporate these things into at least some of your days? Or were you too busy working to fit them in? How can you do things differently next week so that these valuable things don't fall by the wayside?

Having more money doesn't guarantee more happiness

Happiness is love, and per the Beatles, money can't buy it. ~@justinsreality

Money enables us to pursue our passions and survive but in itself can't create permanent true happiness that makes our souls smile. ~@ebear42

Money creates happiness to those who have no idea of what happiness is. To be happy only requires inner and outer peace. ~@LeonelFranco

Money means nothing without humanity. ~@KasunWeer

In my first-hand experience lots of money tears families apart and makes people lose sight of what's important and become miserable. ~@Thearetical

Researchers who analyzed data from the German Socio-Economic Panel recently found that a big indicator of happiness is whether or not someone works the amount of hours per week that he'd like to work. I can personally vouch for this one. If you're happiest when you have time for a hobby or even just relaxing, but you're maintaining a seventy-hour workweek, you will inevitably feel dissatisfied, regardless of how much money you're taking in. That money won't change the fact that you're not living your life in accordance with your priorities and values. This may seem like a no-brainer, but we often do irrational things in the pursuit of more.

There's some interesting research that shows we tend to adjust our spending based on the earners just above us, even if we can't afford to do so. According to Robert H. Frank, author of *Falling Behind: How Rising Inequality Harms the Middle Class*, extremely wealthy people shift the frame of reference for all other earners. When the rich get richer and upgrade their massive houses, the earners just below feel the need go bigger, and it cascades down the economic ladder. Our society ends up with a lot of people buying houses farther away from work to get more value for their dollar, commuting longer hours, borrowing more, saving less, and spending beyond their means.

If most of us work ourselves to the bone and spend both the money we have and the money we don't—and the things we buy require time and maintenance, distracting us from what we actually want to do with our time—it stands to reason that buying may create more stress than it's worth. Accordingly, having more money, which leads to buying more things, can actually negatively impact happiness. Let's think for a minute how financial abundance can soak up time and energy if we use that money to buy stuff.

You have more money so you buy a larger house. You now have to maintain the property—watering and caring for the lawn; heating it in the winter and cooling it in the summer; sinking money into the pool for chemicals, vacuuming, water, replacement filters, and maintenance; and paying increased property taxes and homeowners insurance, even more for the latter if you *do* have said pool, since it presents an accident risk. You need to finance repair work inside the home—such as potentially more backed-up toilets and busted pipes with each additional bathroom you have. You'll likely upgrade some of your other possessions to be consistent with this new large house—get a huge flat-screen TV, top-of-the-line appliances, and perhaps a second mortgage. You probably get a more expensive car. Those monthly payments increase, as does that insurance. Repair work becomes more expensive.

Your children, if you have them, want to do as you do, not as you say—if you even speak of frugality anymore. So they also want more expensive cell phones, designer clothes, and electronics for their bedrooms. That doesn't even factor into the equation all the other costs associated with parenting. In its 2009 annual report, the Agriculture Department estimated that the (almost) total cost of raising a child born in that year was nearly a quarter of a million dollars. That was with childcare, education, health care, and transportation—but this doesn't reflect the cost of college tuition.

All the while, you're struggling emotionally and physically to sustain these expenses, both because you've become accustomed to a certain lifestyle and because losing them might feel like losing control. Giving up what you've gained might seem like a loss of power or an admission that you've failed. And there's something magical about spending money—a quick endorphin rush that makes you feel temporarily euphoric. Yet that small high from acquiring something new can't compensate for the fact that you've made a choice to suffocate your hours in the pursuit of more, leaving little time for the things that actually fulfill you.

If you get stressed by all these increased responsibilities and the pressure of maintaining an exhausting schedule to meet them, you can expect health complications. Chronic stress can lead to depression, hyperthyroidism, ulcers, headaches, insomnia, memory loss, hair loss, and bowel disease. If you eat your feelings (or if you just eat more because more always seems better than less), you put yourself at risk for cardiovascular disease, stroke, diabetes, fatty liver disease, gallbladder disease, deep vein thrombosis, and a host of other illnesses. You might also start smoking or drinking excessively to deal with the related worry, which each has its own associated health risks.

Of course, you might not choose any destructive habit to temper the persistent sense of tension that comes from overextending yourself. You might choose a healthy habit like meditation or yoga to release that stress from your body. But wouldn't life be a lot easier if you simply avoided creating that stress in the first place—if instead of filling your space with things and your time with tasks to afford and maintain those things, you found a more direct path to what you really want?

So often we think what we want is where we're headed—that magical someday when we pay off all the bills and can spend a lot with less worry. But what if that day doesn't come? It sounds morbid to say it, but the reality is that we never know what might happen in the future. If you effectively sacrifice now for later, what happens when later you're not healthy? Or later, the people you love and would like to share your fortune with are no longer around? What happens if later you realize what you really want is what you always had but ignored while earning, spending, and juggling your finances?

Money can be a massive distraction from what truly matters in our lives. Sometimes having less is a blessing we don't recognize until we're drowning in more.

Minimize to reduce work- and stuff-related stress.

If you're feeling overwhelmed by the schedule you've created:

Fill in the blank: *I am willing to gamble ____ hours per week in the hope of becoming wealthy one day.* Make no mistake about it: trading your hours now for potential wealth later will always be a gamble. For every workaholic who became successful, there are limitless others who failed. Sometimes rewards aren't reciprocal to efforts or talents—so you need to know going in what you're willing to risk.

This isn't meant to be discouraging; it's meant to be a reality check. If you were to push yourself fourteen hours a day for twenty years, achieve massive success, and then learn that you have two months to live, would you be happy with how you spent those twenty years? If the answer is no, ascertain right now: how many hours are you willing to devote to the pursuit of wealth, and how many do you want to spend in some other way?

Restructure your schedule to reduce your workload. Now that you know how much time you want to have for those other things you identified as valuable, ask yourself: How can you scale back to allow yourself more time for those things? Can you set firmer boundaries for off days? Can you talk to your boss about shifting certain responsibilities? Can you increase your efficiency and reduce distractions so that you get more done in less time? Parkinson's Law states that work expands to fill the time allotted for its completion—can you allot yourself less time?

Identify areas where you can reduce your spending. This is the other part of the equation: if you're working less, you'll need to spend less. Can you

Continues

go car-less and start riding a bike or using public transportation? Do you really need an expensive cable package, or can you do with just basic or no cable at all? Can you drop that expensive gym membership and start jogging outside instead? Go through every bill and ask yourself: *how can I slash or eliminate this?* The less you have to maintain, the more time and energy you'll have for the things that really matter to you.

You need enough money to provide for necessities

You need security to be happy, therefore, you need enough money to feel secure. Having more won't make you happier. ~@**Innerfoodzilla**

You need money for even the most basic needs. Without money, there is worry. With worry, there is no true happiness. ~@**¡Livin**

Money is needed to have a roof over your head. Spirituality makes a person, not money. ~@**cinfynwine**

We created a system where the basics aren't free. However, the need is infinitesimal compared to the want. ~@**belindavmunoz**

In the current form of society you actually do need money to be happy. Total amounts of either do not correlate. ~@**ChrisMAlexander**

In his book *Stumbling on Happiness*, Daniel Gilbert suggests that money is only important insofar as it meets our basic needs. Once we surpass a certain amount of money, it doesn't actually make us happier, since money can't buy all the things that lead to long-term happiness: self-esteem, love, emotional security, or any of the other intangibles that lead to personal fulfillment. According to Gilbert, money can make a big difference if we move from a lower-class to a middle-class income, since $50,000 affords a much more comfortable lifestyle than $10,000 does. Once we reach a certain number of extra zeros in our paycheck, though, it's unlikely we'll experience any greater joy in life.

Economists Angus Deaton and Daniel Kahneman seem to have found that magic number for those of us living in the United States: $75,000. They analyzed a survey of 450,000 Americans, collected for the 2008 and 2009 Gallup-Healthways Well-Being Index, to see if happiness increased with income. Those people *did* feel happier as their salaries rose, but only up to $75K. Their findings support Gilbert's theory—people who earned double that amount didn't report being twice as happy. The constant—which we likely didn't need research to show—is that it's hard to be happy when you feel like you're just barely staying afloat; and it's infinitely more difficult if you don't know how you're going to pay rent or take care of your family. In a challenged economy, when many people are making just enough to get by, is it possible to be happy?

Right out of college, I performed in a production of *A Christmas Carol* with equity actors who made a living on the regional theater circuit. I was still living at home and only doing the play for fun and experience. My fellow actors were self-sufficient adults with bills and responsibilities and making less than $400 per week—less than I would later collect on unemployment and, annually, far less than $75,000. I never saw any flashy cars, I suspect they all lived in modest homes and apartments, and I'm pretty sure every one of them brought Tupperware-filled lunches (except Bob Cratchit, whose wife was a lawyer). It wasn't Broadway. It wasn't Hollywood. It certainly wasn't glamorous. But that didn't seem to even slightly matter; these were some of the most joyous, most vibrant people I've ever met in my life. As the ghost of Christmas Present told me, "I get to play and pretend for a living." They loved what they were doing, and that joy and fulfillment more than justified the sacrifices, perceived or real, that they made.

Recognizing that, I decided then that I didn't want to perform for a living. At the time, that income didn't feel like nearly enough for the life I wanted to live. I wanted to see the world, move around a lot, have tons of exciting adventures, and never feel trapped in one place, job, or way of being. Yet in this last decade, while earning an average salary of $30,000, I *have* seen the world, moved around a lot, had tons of exciting adventures, and jumped ship from more jobs, homes, and ways of being than I ever would have thought possible. Somehow, without having anywhere near what I once thought was necessary, I lived the life I was chasing. I didn't always realize it and appreciate it in the moment. In fact, I often missed out on amazing possibilities while mourning what I didn't have. But it was all there all along, just like that beautiful Kansas Dorothy finally recognized as where she wanted to be.

The people I wanted to meet were always outside my door. The sights I wanted to see were just a bus or ferry ride away. The life I wanted to live was always within my reach. I have always had enough. But for too long, I was just too busy waiting for it to recognize it was already with me. And I was too busy thinking *I* wasn't enough to accept the moment for what it was. It wasn't until I decided to find enough in the world in front of me that I started feeling fortunate. It wasn't until I realized there was nowhere to get to and nothing to acquire that I started engaging with the world and using the enough I already had.

There is something to enjoy and appreciate in every moment, if you're willing to stop resisting what is. "

Time truly is the ultimate currency, and we waste it if we're too busy bemoaning what we lack and chasing abundance, trying to leverage the secret to attracting it. The *real* secret is the knowledge that right now you have everything you need to make a choice for happiness. You might not have a job you love, but you have the ability to look for something new and put yourself out there to seize that possibility. You might not have a job at all, but you have the capacity to simplify while you get through a rough patch and to use that time to connect with the things that never cost a dime to enjoy. You may not love everything you need to do to get by, but there is something to enjoy and appreciate in every moment, if you're willing to stop resisting what is.

I'll admit this is something that's nearly impossible to do on a 24/7 basis. I love running *TinyBuddha.com*; I feel purposeful and proud of myself every day for making the choice to run this site, even though it requires a large time commitment outside the work I do to financially support myself. But I've realized that the old adage isn't definitively true—just because you do what you love, that doesn't guarantee the money will follow. It's *more likely* you'll succeed doing something you love, since you'll be passionate enough to keep going in the face of obstacles and disappointment, but it isn't guaranteed. Some days, I imagine what life would be like if I could only do *Tiny Buddha* and drop the work that doesn't matter to me as much—or even more fantastic, how amazing it would be to pay off my parents' mortgage and buy homes on both coasts. It's human to wonder what else is out there and if maybe just a little more would make life better. To some extent, that's a good thing. Dissatisfaction is the mother of innovation, and we need to keep creating new visions, possibilities, and ways of being if we're committed to growing and evolving.

John D. Rockefeller once answered the question "How much is enough?" with "Just a little bit more." I suspect most of us will feel this way on and off throughout our lives, just like sometimes we'll have more and sometimes we'll have less. Everything ebbs and flows. Maybe that's okay. We don't need to feel permanently satisfied. We just need to know we have a choice from day to day as to how we feel about who we're being and what we're doing. We can decide that even though there's something we're working toward, what we have in the moment is enough to be happy.

Identify what is enough.

If you always feel like you need more than what you have:

Make a list of your top needs. What do you need to thrive and feel happy in life? What conditions and possessions are absolutely essential to your well-being? What do you need to feel secure, comfortable, engaged, fulfilled, and content? Think about physical needs, like your home and your car; emotional needs, like support from friends and a connection at work; and fulfillment needs, including purpose, accomplishment, and growth. Be as specific as possible in every category. Will any car do? Do you need a certain quantity of or quality in interactions? Does your purpose need to involve a specific job?

Identify which needs emerge from the comparison game. Are there certain things you think you need to have just because other people have them? If no one else had a nicer car than yours, would the one you have seem completely sufficient? If everyone lived in smaller houses than yours, would yours suddenly seem like more than enough? If all of your friends were living comfortably and happily on $20,000 annually, would doing something you love for $30,000 per year seem sufficient? This helps you create an internal benchmark of what is truly enough for you—one not based on what other people have or think, but based on what actually contributes to your sense of fulfillment and joy.

Highlight the needs that don't cost any money. For me, these include quality time with the people I love, opportunities to be spontaneous without any concrete plans, and abundant time to see and enjoy the sunshine.

Continues

Measure your desires against your sense of enough. There's nothing wrong with striving for things and accomplishments if you really want them. The key is to learn to recognize what you actually want and what you only think you want that will end up distracting you from what's important to you. If there's something you think you need to have, ask yourself: Is this outside the realm of what you determined to be enough? Will striving for it somehow hinder your ability to enjoy the items you highlighted?

What we really want is freedom

Money represents liberty; it's that quality that draws people to it. So the question is: Does one need liberty to be happy? ~@cre813

Without money, you don't have the freedom to pursue all that you want and help other people to do the same. ~@brendaclayson

Our society is ruled by money. It's the only way to escape unnecessary worries. ~@DeputyBob1

It's a double-sided coin. Happiness is free. The freedom to celebrate happiness includes the joy of spending money. ~@_LiveInspired_

We need money as it gives freedom of choice. It is a tool but money itself cannot give us happiness, only a delusional one. ~@audrey_drunk

When you think about the times when you've pushed your-self toward abundance, when you've fantasized about life on the other side of your to-do list, odds are you can boil what you're chasing down to one thing: to feel happy—more specifically, to feel a sense of freedom. That unifies us all. It's the ribbon we visualize at the end of the rat race. It's right in the Declaration of Independence: we're all entitled to life, liberty, and the pursuit of happiness. *Dictionary.com* defines *liberty* as "the freedom from con-trol, interference, obligation, restriction, and hampering conditions; the power or right of doing, thinking, and speaking, according to choice."

But we don't always feel like we have the power to choose. We might have independence, but sometimes we need to depend on other people, as when finances are tight. We might be free from government control, but we're not always free to spend our days how we choose—at least not right away. It takes time, trial and error, and sustained effort to earn the luxury of doing what we love for money. We may be allowed the pursuit of happiness, but the fact that we've been taught that happiness is something to chase and obtain actually decreases our odds of ever being happy, since it can't possibly exist in a time other than the present. Freedom implies doing what you want when you want, but sometimes we just can't get what we want. While it might seem logical to stress about all the things we can't do and have, and spend our time scheming to eventually do and have them, this leaves us with very little time to create the situations that actually would give us the feelings we're chasing.

The things we want all come down to feelings—whether you want to feel proud, engaged, connected, fulfilled, satisfied, or challenged, and through it all, happy. Those feelings don't only exist in tomorrow. They're not exclusive to the targets you've imagined, the goals you've visualized, or the narrow definition of freedom you've established in your own head and heart.

True freedom is freedom from your own self-imposed limitations. It's the ability to accept situations as they are, in all their abundance and all their lack, and focus on the abundance. Freedom means waking up and deciding to do something today, with exactly what you have, for your happiness. And if you have to use some time doing something you don't love, you get to be free from your own internal judgment, narration, and dissatisfied self-harassment—free to find enjoyable pieces in a less than enjoyable job because you've accepted the moment for what it is. Freedom is choosing to be happy with the way things are now, even if you're working toward something different tomorrow, because today is all you're guaranteed. As Jean-Paul Sartre wrote, "Freedom is what you do with what's been done to you."

I can't say I wouldn't buy more if I had more money, but I know I wouldn't buy stuff. I would likely buy experiences— vacations with my boyfriend, trips with both our families, and adventures with friends I love. I'd learn Italian in Italy, practice yoga on the beach in Costa Rica, and meditate in Bhutan, where they measure their nation's success in GNH— gross national happiness. I fantasize about this sometimes, as I imagine my boyfriend does when he buys his weekly lottery tickets. Then I remind myself: I might not be able to go to Italy tomorrow, but I can learn Italian right now. I may not have the money to take a yoga retreat in Costa Rica, but I live in Los Angeles—I can do my downward dog on multiple gorgeous beaches. And I might not have the means to get into Bhutan, but I don't need to wait for a plane ticket to start measuring my success in gross individual happiness.

None of us do.

POSSIBILITIES

HOW CAN YOU MAKE
EACH DAY COUNT?

~~~~~~~~~~~~~~~~~~~~~~~~~~

This seems to be the question the other ones dance around: how to live each day—and life itself—to the fullest? We can thank Roman lyric poet Horace for the popular phrase *carpe diem*, which he included in a poem in 23 BCE. Loosely translated, it means "seize the day," or in the context of Horace's poem, "pluck the day, putting as little trust as possible in tomorrow." It's a mentality a lot of us don't think to adopt until we come face-to-face with mortality, our own or someone else's—and then once we realize it, we often let our awareness get the better of us. The same mental faculties that understand the present is all that's guaranteed whittle away at today with analysis, worry, and judgment. Sometimes we get so bogged down trying to make every day count that we miss out on the day in the process.

Conventional wisdom suggests we should live every day as if it's our last, which isn't exactly the best advice. It might make sense if each day occurred independently of every other, but they do, in fact, connect to form a complete life. Accepting that tomorrow might not exist doesn't change the fact that it quite likely will. If you live the average life expectancy of seventy-eight years, you have 341,640 days—meaning that a tomorrow will arrive 341,639 times. If we lived every day as though we'll literally die at the end of it, a lot of us might assume a hedonistic lifestyle—we'd eat, drink, be merry, and drain our savings and 401(k)s in the process. We probably wouldn't work toward any long-term goals. Why bother when today is all there is? Why work harder for an early retirement when retirement isn't on our radar? Why go back to school to advance our career or increase our earning potential when we only need enough for our pleasure today?

To live life to the fullest, we need to balance two simultaneous needs: the desire to reach our full potential and the instinct to enjoy today. We need to allow ourselves every opportunity to blossom over time while creating possibilities for joy in the moment. Sometimes we have to delay gratification but that doesn't mean we can't feel gratified in whatever circumstances we choose.

This year has arguably been one of the fullest of my life. In February, when my unemployment benefits expired, I took on another work-from-home web writing job and set four goals for my future: secure a book deal, transition to self-employment, move in with Ehren, and spend at least a month in Boston with my family. I decided that accomplishing that first goal would give me the green light to do the rest—that if I could just get the book deal, I'd quit my job, move out of my place, and give myself permission to disconnect from my West Coast life for travel and a prolonged East Coast stay. That's precisely what happened in May 2010.

Once I got the contract for this book in my hands, I dropped everything else and started making plans for a summer adventure, including time in Vegas, Sedona, New York, and Cape Cod, as well as a month with my family in Boston. I essentially tossed a wrecking ball into my life, and then decided to let the ruins simmer while I played and explored for a while. This may sound like an act of bravery, but remember: deconstruction is the foundation of my comfort zone. I've wiped the slate clean many times before. Some people thrive on consistency; I've always felt far more comfortable with none, my life a tabula rasa that I can pretend will one day be written with only good things.

The real act of bravery was deciding to enjoy the leap instead of dwelling on whether or not it was smart to have faith—to find reward from moment to moment instead of seeing the risk as a means to a better end. That's always what it's been about for me. Everything I did, everything I wanted and grabbed, and everything I eventually released was an attempt to create a perfect life that would be worth fully enjoying. This summer I decided to appreciate what *is* instead of worrying about what might be.

I watched my sister's face light up when she saw the Vegas strip for the first time and remembered how beautiful the world is when you're not obsessing about yourself. I meditated in a Sedona vortex, like a tiny pebble nestled high above the vast red-rock canyon. I slurped oysters with my dad on the Cape and relaxed poolside with my mom while we sipped vodka and sodas and twirled our hair in the same compulsive way. I climbed to the top of the Eiffel Tower with Ehren and his family and, thankfully, didn't hyperventilate from excessive height-induced panic.

And I explored Thoreau's cabin in the woods with my brother after a hike we'd talked about completing for years but had never made the time to take. Standing in that cramped space where Thoreau lived alone for two years and two months—focusing only on the sound of silence, the serene view outside the window, and my gratitude for time with my brother—I understood simplicity more clearly than ever before. It has little to do with access to shingles and bricks and everything to do with the capacity to be fully where we are.

It wasn't hard to do that while traveling and using other people's time-shares, or staying in my parents' house. Sleeping in a bed I didn't have to buy, eating food I didn't have to work for, and anticipating relaxing days with the family members who missed me easily evoked a sense of appreciation. What I didn't know was how to carry my mindfulness with me through the fall when life got busy again. If the past was any indication, it was entirely likely I'd crawl into my turtle shell with to-do lists lining the interior and only occasionally pop out my head to reinsert my caffeine drip. I very well could get tangled in obligations, responsibilities, possibilities, and stresses and eventually collapse under the weight of my ambitions and perfectionism. I saw the meticulous writing on the wall and hoped that maybe I wouldn't have to choose between a peaceful today and a limitless tomorrow.

At first, I let my plans and action steps sweep me away in a tornado of busyness. On week one back home, I was drowning in smart goals, thinking maybe the smartest thing was to have no goals at all. It was so much easier to feel satisfied while traveling, when I had nothing to do but be me with the people I love. It was easier to be me in a time without objectives, when I didn't have to worry about not doing a good enough job, or doing my best and failing anyway.

Then I decided to consider a new possibility: maybe I could have a lot to do without stressing about where it was leading. Maybe the most exciting possibility was the possibility of being and enjoying things exactly as they are even while working toward what could be. There will always be twenty-four hours in a day. Whether or not those hours feel overwhelming and harried is completely up to us. It's taken me several years, multiple exhausted panic attacks, and far too many Red Bulls to realize it, but it is possible to work hard without completely losing myself in the tasks. It is possible to get everything done without pushing through each moment, chasing a carrot on a stick that will always be just slightly out of reach.

Over the last few months, I've written from coffee shops and the beach instead of creating a me-shaped dent in my couch; I've bisected the workday with hikes, burrito runs, and exploratory drives in my new neighborhood; and I've given myself permission to do nothing when there's still lots to be done because, as my own boss, I am the only person who can tell me to stop and take a break.

Today Ehren asked me if I wanted to play basketball with him down the street. At 5'1" and with the upper body strength of a toddler and the coordination of a basset hound on skis, I instinctively mumbled no and continued clacking away on my laptop keys. After all, I'm still not finished with this book and my inbox won't empty itself. Then something compelled me to stop and try something new. So what if he destroyed me on the court and I felt bored in about twenty minutes? Just getting outside was a choice to open up to possibilities.

After we arrived, he tried to teach me to play defense, which I tailored into a combination of shirt grabbing, tackling, and forced piggybacking right before he went to shoot. For a while I sprinted, dribbled, and pretended to learn, but I didn't do that because I wanted to be able to play basketball beyond the HORSE game I grew up playing with my brother. I did it because I know he loves the sport, and sharing it with him seemed special, albeit clumsy and a little embarrassing.

Like clockwork, I lost interest just shy of a half-hour in, but that was actually perfect timing. A real game was developing across the way, which Ehren could join, and an impossibly green patch of land was pulling me like a grassy magnetic field.

As I nestled myself into the earth beneath a mammoth tree, noticing shards of sunlight on my arms from the space between the branches and dozens of shadows strolling across the lawn, I felt blissful and calm. It was a lot like the way I usually felt when I quit an unsatisfying job or purged myself of all responsibilities. It was the same sense of lightness and ease, and yet I knew there was still so much I didn't know—if my work was paying off, if I was working smart or just hard, or if the life I was creating would work for me better than the one that I had prior. In this moment of time, everything was working right, and yet the moment didn't depend on my circumstances. I felt a genuine sense of freedom, and it had nothing to do with what I did or had to do.

I suddenly realized I could have been anywhere. That tree could have sat outside my parents' house, where it's undoubtedly freezing this autumn day; it could have grown from an unlikely sliver of earth in Times Square, like a beacon of stability amid the urban chaos; it could have sprung through the pavement of the Golden Gate Bridge, placing me smack-dab in the middle of swerving traffic; it could even have been a prop on a movie set near my current home in LA. Regardless of where that tree sat, where I sat beneath it, and what went on around it, I would have felt satisfied with being. My peace didn't depend on a specific locale or activity. It grew from a place deep inside me—a part of me that consented to be part of the world, even as it changes like the seasons around me. A part of me that had finally learned that fully living starts with fully being.

John Lennon said, "Time you enjoyed wasting was not wasted." While I've learned there is nothing more valuable than the capacity to value your own time, I have to admit it's not easy to do on an ongoing basis—both because life inevitably involves struggle and because the mind likes to cling to problems, stress about them, and experience even more of them while planning to avoid them.

There's no reason to look back on a happy moment as somehow misallocated, but this idea does bring up some questions. Is enjoyment the sole barometer for a life lived fully? If we can simply take solace in enjoying our time, then how do we know when to push through discomfort to open ourselves up to something new? At what point do we sacrifice our enjoyment for someone else's or for the greater good? Looking back on the moments that we didn't enjoy, should we ascertain that they were all wasted? And is enjoyment as simple as choosing to enjoy or does it require some type of advanced planning?

With these thoughts in mind, I asked on Twitter, "How can you make each day count?"

Show up every day

Make each day count by forgetting the past and not expecting the future. ~@Scottstimo

To make each day count, simply realize that it will never again be today after today. ~@jLivin

Be present in the moment and observe the wonderful things happening around you. ~@littlemsgg

Stay present to how very small we are in the universe, yet how beautiful. Live in the beauty. ~@rmcoplon

Live life with love and compassion. Live it like it's your last day and live it to the maximum. Life is sweet so make it sweeter! ~@lifeofhappiness

If you agree that time is precious and each day matters, you could surmise that you squandered the days that you spent bored, isolated, angry, resigned, or in any other way disconnected from joy. From there, you can get caught up in what you should have done and let even more time slip away while you rehash, assess, and judge how and who you've been.

One of the most common misconceptions in life is that what we did yesterday has to somehow dictate what we can do or be today. It doesn't. We never have to be limited by who we've been. At any time, we can decide to be or do something different and totally redirect the trajectory of our lives. In order to do this, we need to know that we are the only one keeping score, and we truly can wipe the slate clean not only on any morning but also at any time. The "day" when we decide to live out loud can start at any moment.

The late John Wooden, a UCLA basketball coach, once received a piece of now-famous advice from his father: make each day your masterpiece. It's an interesting choice of words, because artists are famously perfectionist about their work. In my mid-twenties, I modeled for life-drawing classes in an attempt to heal my relationship with my body. I never met a single painter who felt satisfied with the canvas at the end of a class. There was always the thought of another glimpse at the model, another stroke, or another touch to bring the work to life. Paul Gardner wrote, "A painting is never finished. It simply stops in interesting places." The same is true of our days. There will always be more we could have done, and yet to truly live the next day to the fullest, we need to let go of worries about what we did or didn't do the day before.

Perhaps the best advice is *not* to make every day your masterpiece, but instead to come to your canvas every day. Just show up. Instead of dwelling on what you didn't do yesterday, do something about it now. Instead of analyzing the choices you could have made, make better choices now. Instead of giving yourself a hard time for what you should have done, realize you did the best you could and decide to do the best you can now. At the end of your life, the moments that you will remember won't be the ones when you sat judging your life and yourself. It won't be a montage of times when you curled up alone, contemplating the mistakes you made or the things you should have done. The memories you'll have will be visions of action—the activities and events you enjoyed, the time you spent with people you love, and the moments when you engaged with life in brave and daring ways.

I've recently started jogging at a park near my home where there's a track, a field, and a playground. Every time I go, I fight with the instinct to stop running and instead jump on a swing and wait for someone to come give me an underdog—less because I want to engage in childlike play and more because I always told myself I'd never run unless I was being chased. I just don't enjoy it, but I took up the hobby because it was a simple, free way to exercise, and that seemed like my only option.

It takes me several minutes to get from my starting point on the track to the point directly in front of the playground, and only a few seconds to pass that little oasis of fun. It's a struggle every time as I notice waddling toddlers, rambunctious preschoolers, and even chubby little babies perched in strollers, looking carefree and oblivious to the fun they're missing. The other day, I saw a little girl sitting by herself in the sand. She was tossing it around in handfuls—getting it on her clothes, in her hair, and on the adjacent cement. If it had been a floor, I'd be desperate to Swiffer it. If she'd been my child, I'd feel the need to disinfect her.

In a way, I should be grateful for my OCD cleaning instincts because they eventually compelled me to stop running and take a closer look. I sat myself on a swing to the left of that child and stared peripherally—didn't want to alarm a nanny or parent. I was fascinated. She had a Band-Aid on her head. I imagined she must have toppled over the day before, learning to walk maybe. Or perhaps she already knew how but, like all toddlers, she wanted to move faster than her drumstick-like limbs would take her. Regardless of what might have happened yesterday, she was completely immersed in the tactile experience of playing with the sand. She wasn't reacting to yesterday's boo-boo; she was getting messy in today's slice of fun. She appeared amused, entertained, and even fascinated by what she could make with her pail and the dirt. The idea of not coming out to play probably had never crossed her mind. In her resilience, enthusiasm, and filthy mindfulness, she was a masterpiece.

Obviously there's a lot to be said for no longer being a toddler, including more socially acceptable bathroom habits and the capacity to assess feelings before wailing or having a tantrum. But a childlike way of being can be empowering. Kids explore the world with eyes of wonder. They give hugs like they're going out of style. They get messy without worrying about losing control. They say what's on their mind and then leave it behind them. They're endlessly amused by the simplest things—an interestingly shaped rock, a snow cone on a hot day, or a paper towel holder that could be a million different things, from an instrument to a telescope to a house for fairies. They roll with new ideas like there's no alternative to being creative. And they rarely choose to sit around feeling bad when they could get out and find some fun. They know that every day won't be fun, but the only way to find out is to take a chance and go.

Create childlike presence.

If you frequently feel like you're just going through the motions:

Give yourself time to explore without any objective or agenda. This might mean taking a walk without anywhere specific to go, or learning something new even though you don't actually need that skill. Simply allow yourself a window to forget about time and instead follow wherever your interests and instincts guide you. Think of this as adult playtime and practice so you can fully show up more often. Exploring is the destination.

Let yourself get messy. This doesn't mean dump sand on your head, although it can, if that's your choice. It simply means loosen up! Resist the urge to wield control over every aspect of how people see you. If you feel like trying something new but you're afraid you'll look silly, do it anyway. It's a whole lot easier to be present when you're not suffocating your presence with fears.

See the new in the familiar. You may very well see a lot of the same things from one day to the next, especially if you follow a routine for work. Make it a point to notice the things that you would otherwise tune out—how there are new flowers growing in front of the house you walk by every day, or the way more people are having lunch at the restaurant near your office. It's difficult to notice these tiny changes when you're caught up in your head. When you actively choose to look for them, you will naturally be more present within your surroundings.

Take risks

Do something different, completely unnatural to what you would usually do. After a week, "usual" stops existing! ~@ArnaudJolois

Step out of your comfort zone, take at least one small risk, and do at least one thing that no one says thank you for. ~@AlexaEldredge

Grab every chance with both hands. It might not be there tomorrow. ~@squishy3000

Don't live each day as if it's your last—live each day as if it's your first. ~@cobbwt

Look back with respect and humor, forward with delight and wonder, and enjoy the little things along the way. ~@JosetteN

With all this talk of being childlike, it's worth mentioning that there are certain faculties we develop in adulthood that serve us well. The other day I read about research related to adolescent brain chemistry and risks. According to cognitive neuroscientist Russell Poldrack, teenagers are especially sensitive to the pleasure sensations they experience when something turns out better than they anticipated. Poldrack and his colleagues at the University of Texas suggest it has to do with *positive prediction error*—when you expect an experience will end badly but instead you end up pleasantly surprised. Apparently, fourteen- to-nineteen-year-olds receive a greater release of dopamine—the chemical associated with the brain's reward center—when something that could have been catastrophic ends well. This could explain why teens are more likely to experiment with drugs, binge drink, or drive way over the speed limit despite knowing the related risks; the possibility of reward outweighs the fear of consequences. In a very literal way, teens have a lot less fear than adults do.

As adults, most of us are far less likely to take dangerous risks, which is a good thing, so long as we don't let the pendulum swing too far the other way. I've met a lot of people who seem to swaddle themselves in bubble wrap each day, trying to avoid the possible bumps, bruises, and aches associated with vulnerability. One friend of mine actually told me she has *decidophobia*—the fear of making decisions. She has a ton of regrets about her past, most centered on having missed out on life while she was in a long, unhealthy relationship. She's so terrified of making another decision that she'll later consider wrong that she feels paralyzing anxiety whenever she has to make any decision—even the smallest one. I've seen her have panic attacks over what to do on a Friday night. Sometimes this means she ends up doing nothing at all, feeling secure in the knowledge she didn't make the wrong choice. But no choice is still a choice.

The truth is we can't ever know how something is going to turn out once we take a leap. We may like to think we knew after the fact—the hindsight bias thing—but we can't know. All we can do is trust our gut, find the courage to take action, and then trust that if it doesn't turn out how we hoped, we can handle it. We can take whatever strokes we've put on the canvas and work with them to make something beautiful.

It's not an easy thing to do, and it's why a lot of us get stuck waiting for the right time to act or for some type of sign that it's okay to act at all. When I was deeply entrenched in a waiting place, a voyeur to everyone else's lives, someone told me that life is like driving a car. If you were to get lost, you wouldn't just pull over and wait it out, intellectualizing what the roads might look like in different directions and questioning whether or not you're really qualified or ready to go down certain streets. You'd either start driving and gauge as you go, or you'd get directions and trust them enough to get back on your journey. If you still don't like where you're going, you ask for more help and get right back behind the wheel.

The key is choosing to go—to see what's down those streets. To take a chance. To stop waiting for a guarantee that you know what you're doing and start realizing no one does. We are all learning as we go. No one has it all figured out. No one goes to bed at night feeling fully confident in her decisions. No one knows for sure that a risk is going to pay off. No one can foresee what's coming. That's the beauty of life. It's not a straight line; it's more like an EKG monitor with peaks and valleys. It's a choose-your-own adventure that we can write as we go. And if we get bored, we can pull out the page and start again.

We can also trust that as we move forward and learn, we'll be able to take even smarter risks. According to Howard H. Stevenson, coauthor of *Make Your Own Luck: 12 Practical Steps to Taking Smarter Risks in Business*, "Every decision is a bet. The question is, how can you make better bets?" Though the book is geared to business-related risks, it offers wisdom to improve our "predictive intelligence" in all areas of our lives. We can get clear about our intentions—what exactly it is we're hoping to create. We can make efforts to understand possible outcomes, so we'll be able to stay open and keep moving as we experience twists and turns. We can connect with other people on our journey so that we're not alone with our risks. And we can prepare well in case a risk doesn't pay off—have a plan B, so to speak—so we can cut our losses and move on if necessary.

One of the perks of running a website that publishes posts related to happiness is that I have access to the analytics of inspiration. I've noticed that some of the most popular posts on *TinyBuddha.com* are the ones related to risks and possibilities. Someone quits his job to pursue what he really loves or someone takes a sabbatical to travel the world, and the retweets go through the roof. We all want to find the courage to do something that we only dream about—even if it doesn't involve making a massive change in our lives. We all want the motivation to do one of the things we only talk about—to actually write the book instead of just imagining it will be a best seller, or to make the film instead of stopping with the fantasy of an Oscar. Sometimes we're just too afraid of what might go wrong to plow full speed ahead toward everything that could go right.

The truth is, the future could unfold in any number of ways—it could be everything we imagined, or nothing like we'd hoped. Even so, the latter could be pleasantly surprising. We can't possibly know until we're there. It's natural to be somewhat afraid of the unknown, and a little caution is healthy. What's important is that we learn to take smart risks in spite of that little voice that says, *Go back. It's too hard. It's not worth it.* When we're honest with ourselves, we know more often than not, it's worth the risk.

Get outside your comfort zone.

If you feel like you've been playing it safe and you'd like to make a change:

Identify the big things you dream about but think you can only do when you have more money. This might include backpacking in Europe, taking a trip across the country, or quitting your job to do something that you enjoy far more. Forget about what sounds reasonable—let yourself imagine possibilities, the type of things you'd put on a bucket list to do before you kick the bucket.

Start with acceptable alternatives. There's an astronomically inaccurate but powerful quote that reads, "Reach for the moon. Even if you miss, you'll land among the stars." Even though the stars are actually farther away, the point is that if you try, you may not get where you wanted to go, but you'll get closer than you are now—and it might be equally amazing. Landing among the stars is also a good way to ease into living the life you dream about. If you can't afford to backpack through Europe, can you start with a shorter trip somewhere else you want to go? If you can't quit your job and pursue your dream full-time, can you scale back and start volunteering in your dream field on the weekend?

Commit to making the big things happen. In a post on *TinyBuddha.com* titled "On Making the Unreasonable Possible," Jamie Hoang referred to this concept as "issuing yourself a life ticket." When you get a driving or a parking ticket, even if you don't have money put aside, you find a way to pay it because you have to. Maybe you cut back on luxuries for a while, or sell something, or borrow from someone you love. You do it because not doing it isn't an option. Think in the same terms about the things you really want to do with your life, and find a way. I don't have the answer as to how—that's up to you to find.

Appreciate the highs, the lows, the small things, and the big things

Be thankful you woke up and can go to sleep. ~@thornlord

Practice gratitude. It's the easiest way to feel the love and get perspective. ~@atpce

After waking up each morning, greet each new 24 hours as a present and vow to be present to life. ~@nobodhi

Find a good thing in the bad things thrown to us every day. ~@acceva

Be grateful for what we have, the relationships, the peace, the work we enjoy. Spread the joy around. ~@alwayslovely

When I was younger, I found it annoying when someone told me to be grateful for what I had. It seemed like a moral judgment—like people were trying to guilt me into accepting negative situations by implying good people were thankful they were even alive at all. Gratitude seemed less about recognizing actual good things and deeds and more about feeling indebted for the gift of life. Appreciation wasn't about feeling; it was a virtue I seemed to lack.

I later realized that feeling gratitude is as much a gift to myself as it is the ability to recognize gifts in the world around me. Gratitude isn't about ignoring everything that could be improved; it's about shining a light on what's already working, which creates positive feelings about now while enabling positive plans for later. In a very real way, gratitude is the antidote to fear. Fear views events as insufficient, obstructive, and unfair; gratitude sees circumstances as useful, empowering, and ultimately positive. Fear implies there's something to hide or run from; gratitude suggests there's something to embrace. You can only experience positive emotions and results only when you're willing to be responsible for creating them—that means tapping into the part of you that recognizes the good both in what is and in what can be.

Positive psychology has positioned gratitude as a doorway to emotional well-being. Research shows that people who regularly express gratitude experience less stress, feel more in control, cope better with life's difficulties, and handle change more effectively than do people who don't. They also focus more on dealing with problems than on stewing in bitterness about having them.

Rumi wrote that "being human is a guest house" and our job is to welcome new arrivals, whether they bring joy or sadness. Some guests, like disease and tragedy, seem a lot less worthy of a warm reception than others, but our fear won't change the fact that life will inevitably involve pain.

Refusing to open the door won't send unwelcome guests packing. Once we consent to let them in, we create the possibility of working with them.

A new friend named Alison Miller recently contributed an article to *TinyBuddha.com* about dealing with challenges in life. Alison always dreamed about the freedom of flying, so she decided to pursue aerial acrobatics as a hobby. If you're familiar with Cirque du Soleil, you've seen this activity before—it's the art of dancing and contorting thirty feet in the air with only silk fabric for support. One day while gearing up for flight, Alison accidently rigged the fabric incorrectly. From fifteen feet up, Alison began plummeting to the ground, and she hit it, shattering her wrists, breaking a foot, and fracturing her spinal vertebrae. Although she acknowledged that she wouldn't go back and relive the event, Alison wrote that she would never in a million years trade the personal growth she experienced—the injury became an awakening.

It took her four months to get back to her life, and in that time she often felt frustrated by the regression in dependence. But she also decided to find opportunity within adversity. By choosing to see her challenge as a teacher, she eventually realized that deep down she felt lonely, insecure, and afraid—that she excelled at giving but struggled with receiving. She had been filling her hours with busyness to avoid experiencing the pain of those feelings. This forced hiatus from life provided an ideal opportunity to receive love, caring, and support from other people. She fell again, this time into a deeper understanding of what her life was lacking. By being grateful for what she got, she was able to give herself more of what she needed.

When we think of seizing the day, we're more apt to visualize ourselves dangling from the silk fabric, feeling invigorated and euphoric, than we are to imagine ourselves lying in bed, feeling grateful for falling. The former is obviously a lot more exciting than the latter, but both are choices to live life to the fullest. Living a day fully means maximizing the possibilities within it. That starts with accepting the day as it is and then finding ways to leverage that for a sense of peace and forward momentum. It's about finding value in the way things are and using that awareness both to live mindfully today and to shape tomorrow.

No matter where we stand, there will always be somewhere else that looks a little brighter. It's only natural to want to get to those places. Most of us know that we tend to regret the things we didn't do more than we regret the things we did and, understanding that, we want every opportunity to do the things we want. When we feel held back, we get angry and resistant. The reality is that there will be some days when we soar and others when we have to stand still. We can choose to feel fully alive regardless. Living life to the fullest means realizing there is something to appreciate and enjoy in both flight and stillness—that regardless of what we're doing, we can choose to feel positive emotions about who we're being.

There are still things in my life that I would like to change. I don't believe that everything is a miracle just because life itself is. But I no longer think gratitude has to correlate with specific events in life. Seizing the moment isn't about creating a particular positive outcome. It's about being responsible for nurturing a positive one. Gratitude isn't about being good. It's about recognizing that we can fly regardless of what happens to our wings.

Find possibilities in the hand you've been dealt.

If you don't feel grateful for what's in front of you today:

Actively choose your circumstances. This might sound strange, since I prefaced this by saying that you wouldn't actually want what's in front of you, but the reality is, you have to play the cards you have whether you explain it as the hand you've been dealt or as the hand you've chosen. Instead of consenting to accept this and let things happen to you, actively decide you can handle the challenge and use this to help you make positive things happen. Instead of being the resigned victim in the story of today, be the empowered protagonist.

Look for tiny gifts. You might not feel as though your whole situation is a gift, and that's fine. You don't have to lie to yourself and pretend you love being unemployed or you're happy about being sick. But if you look for them, you can find small opportunities within any set of circumstances—tiny possibilities that hinge on the way things are right now. Unemployment gives you an opportunity to figure out what you really want to do with your time. Sickness gives you a forced hiatus from life and an opportunity to reflect on anything that might not be working for you.

Use the gift in some small way today. Whether today's a day for standing still or for soaring, you can reflect on what you've learned about being the person you want to be and then do something small to accomplish that. If your gift was a reminder to slow down, choose to focus solely on what's in front of you and enjoy it, regardless of your struggles. If the gift was a reminder to be a more active part of your family members' lives, take the time to call them solely to listen and be there for them. In this way, you'll create positive emotions for yourself and for the people around you and, in doing so, set the stage for even more gifts down the line.

Let yourself be

Don't be too hard on yourself. Every day is a different best and a different energy. ~**@YogaStudioSouth**

Do everything that you can and don't fret over what doesn't get done. ~**@Simplylibra**

Trust your instincts and believe in yourself. ~**@Sam_Ho**

Do less. And take every day to grow into being more you and into being inspired. ~@2inspired

When your schedule is busy, don't worry about what you have to do next. Think "Today I'm just doing what I'm doing today." ~@RoisinO

Life may be what happens when we're making other plans, but it's also what happens before and after we make them. Life is every moment, in the striving, the struggling, the accepting, the enjoying, the hurting, the waiting, and the going. Life is every last action and every last choice. Life is both the extraordinary we often chase and the ordinary we ignore while we're running.

It's everything—every day, every hour, every moment, and every second—which can seem overwhelming if you think about life as a whole that's inevitably too short. How can you possibly ensure your life looks beautiful in the end, as you step away from all the dots and see how it shapes up as a complete picture, when you can't possibly know when the end will be? How can you use each day wisely if you don't know how many you've been allocated to complete the task of making your life count? How can you possibly let yourself relax when you can never know for certain what needs to be done or if you're doing it well?

The other day while procrastinating in a coffee shop, I decided to play a little game of Human Concentration. You might remember Concentration from your childhood—the game that requires you to remember upside-down cards that you've previously flipped over so you can later find a match. As I sat clutching a soup bowl–sized coffee cup, I decided to identify congruous feelings in the people around me. I knew that regardless of how inert they may have all seemed, the vast majority of them were going over and over things in their head, as though those thoughts were Baoding balls overwhelming their hands, except without the health benefits. I'd recently seen the premiere of the TV show *Lie to Me*, which centers around our ability to recognize lies by noticing people's microexpressions—the tiny knee-jerk facial expressions that reveal what we're really feeling. So in this moment, I looked for those microexpressions and other body cues. Disconnecting for a bit from my feelings of busy self-importance, I devoted myself to identifying which people were feeling something that someone only a few feet away appeared to be feeling, too.

I saw a man typing so furiously on his laptop it seemed he might be punishing his keyboard. Recognizing his furrowed brow and labored breathing, I imagined he felt overwhelming pressure to get something done. After surveying the room and making a few other observations, I decided a woman near the door was feeling similarly. She was staring at her computer with that same shallow breath and stress-contorted face, apparently considering the implications of an email or task. There they were: two people existing in the exact same space, sharing an external experience while also experiencing something very similar internally, parallel stress over something not of that moment. A man and a woman each struggling under the weight of something that may have seemed insurmountable or at the very least annoyingly difficult—something I imagined concerned getting somewhere good or away from somewhere inadequate. At least that's what they would have been experiencing if they were feeling what *I* did when I made those expressions.

Near the bathroom door a woman was staring at her shoes. Even while looking down, her eyes darted around, as if to catch people who might be looking at her. With her shoulders hunched over and her hands in her pockets, she exuded awkwardness. This, I thought, was a woman who felt insecure—out of place, uncomfortable, and certain she didn't like standing where so many people could see her. Not more than five feet away, I saw a guy sitting across from a girl he appeared to be with. Even while reading something on his computer, he repeatedly crossed his arms, uncrossed them, looked at his companion, looked down, looked back at her, crossed his legs, and uncrossed them. Here was yet another person wanting a certain level of approval and feeling anxious about the potential to not receive it.

While people-watching within a dangerously confined space, an emotion voyeur and apparent amateur psychologist, I eventually fixed my attention on someone who appeared to be staring at me. I doubted he was playing the same bizarre game of feeling observation, but I felt certain he'd figuratively crawled into my brain and was poking around at its inner workings. It was amazing how quickly I shifted from objective and open to subjective and defensive. Then I decided that this was a challenge, and I would not look away first. I would figure him out before he deconstructed me. Maybe he also wanted a break from the work in front of him. Maybe my pheromones wafted his way, and he didn't recognize that I was sitting directly across from the large, albeit gentle, man I call my boyfriend. Or maybe, as his sudden soft smile and head nod revealed, he was simply being within that space and happened to lock eyes with mine. Maybe he wasn't feeling anything but the utter freedom of being.

I've been the furious typer, the consumed reader, the anxious waiter, and the nervous admirer many times before, as I imagine we all have. We've all worked toward goals, pondered the implications of our actions, obsessed over other people's opinions, and wished with every fiber of our being we could control them. We've also sat firmly rooted in a space, fully aware that we can let go of everything that keeps us from being where we are. It might seem like we don't have a choice when we consider everything we want to accomplish, how we want to be perceived, and how productive it seems to think about all that in overlapping thoughts in our heads. But in the end, we always have a choice in what we do right now, both with our minds and with our bodies. At any time, we can decide to be fully where we are. The only way to explore what's possible is to first be willing to be.

CONTROL

WHAT CAN WE
CONTROL IN LIFE?

In life we control only our own thoughts, feelings, emotions, and reactions. Accept more, let go more, react less, enjoy more. ~@**BodaciousLib**

The only things in life we can control are our thoughts—their content and how they make us feel. ~@**tamsinmelissa**

The absolute only thing we can control in life is how we respond to everything we have no control of. ~@**roatanvortex**

We cannot control others, but we can control how we choose to respond and react to others. ~@**angieclifford**

We can control our breath. ~@**sweethartdehart**

We can control how we act in any circumstance. Choosing how we act will always get better results than simply reacting. ~@**positivedoing**

We only control little things in life, what to eat or do tonight. The beauty of life is we can't control the major things. ~@**christiancropes**

Our attitudes, our impulses (positive & negative), our views on the actions of others, our will power, and our ambition. ~@**MelissaRowley**

We can only control what we put into our own body and mind. We should be better to ourselves. ~@**cbruels**

Your intention is always up to you; the rest continually changes with your participation. ~@**nobodhi**

At the height of the economic meltdown in 2009, I read an article on *CNN.com* about the surge in appointments for psychic readings. Faced with uncertainty about career prospects and overall security, many Americans packed away their skepticism and headed to their local clairvoyant, hoping to find comfort in a crystal ball. According to a professor at Columbia Business School, Gita Johar, who studies consumer behavior, the strongest motivation for visiting a psychic is to feel a sense of control.

I understand the allure. Between 1995 and 2007, I spent more than $2,000 on psychic readings. Even as I moved and traveled all around the United States—oftentimes with only a credit card to make ends meet—I kept the number for that tearoom in Boston where I became a teenage Wiccan and scheduled appointments to ask if I was heading in the right direction. I'd talk about my career ambitions and how resistant I felt to being in the rat race. I'd wax poetic about my quest for love, questioning whether or not I was getting closer to finding someone who might validate me. I'd complain about the gut-wrenching inner conflict I felt over wanting to go home to Massachusetts but feeling terrified of giving up just before I found myself or my purpose.

Sometimes I rambled for the full half-hour, leaving little if any time to receive insight. It would have been cheaper to get a therapist, but I'd already been down that road—and what I wanted was a guarantee that everything would be okay. I wanted some type of assurance that I was doing the right things and that I could give myself permission to stop worrying. For a long time, I convinced myself the strangers with the tarot cards gave me the strength to go on; until one day I looked back and realized they never actually gave me any concrete answers. They never predicted where my life was headed or outlined a road map to get there. They merely gave me the illusion of knowing absolute truth. It wasn't the truth that set me free; it was the way I let go when I believed I could trust that I knew the truth.

When I look back on my experiences with *TinyBuddha* *.com* and everything that brought me to it, what I realize is that I feel no less uncertain about the world and my place within it now than I ever did. There has never been a moment in time when I felt like I had discovered that magic bullet, the ultimate answer to happiness, understanding, and wisdom. There's never been a moment when I've felt I have it all figured out. There is still so much that I don't know or understand, and yet I'm liberated having decided to accept that and instead to focus on what I can do right now.

You may never know where you've come from or where you're going, but you can choose what you do with the time you know you have. You can accept that pain is inevitable and save yourself and others a lot of suffering by learning from it all as you go. You'll never be perfect, but if you believe in yourself and commit to new possibilities, you can change, both because you want to and because the world changes around you. Sometimes things will happen that you may never understand, but you have a say in how the future unfolds and how you react to the things you didn't anticipate.

You have a say in how often you cling to negative emotions and how often you let go, giving yourself permission to feel free and happy. You get to choose the things you do each day, even if it doesn't always seem that way. Every day, you can decide to do something to feel meaningful, empowered, happy, and connected. Even if it's something little—*especially* if it's something little. The most beautiful things in life grow from the choice to start with one simple step. You get to choose what you think and feel about it all, whether you create limiting stories about what things mean or you open yourself up to new possibilities you didn't even know to imagine. If one day you don't do so well with being proactive and present, you can start all over, right where you are, without carrying the burden of what's been. You can decide at any time to be reborn.

You can decide at any time that you don't need to have all the answers. You just need to honestly answer the question of what you want to do with your life—who you want to be and what that might look like. In a highly uncertain world, you can reassure yourself that you don't have to know and control everything. You just have to trust that you know enough to take responsibility for now.

50 Things You Can Control Right Now (from *TinyBuddha.com*)

1. How many times you smile.

2. How much effort you exert at work.

3. Your level of honesty.

4. How well you prepare.

5. How you act on your feelings.

6. How often you say, "Thank you."

7. When you pull out your wallet for luxuries.

8. Whether or not you give someone the benefit of the doubt.

9. How you interpret situations.

10. Whether or not you compete with people around you.

11. How often you notice and appreciate small acts of kindness—hint: they're everywhere!

12. Whether you listen or wait to talk.

13. When you walk away from a conversation.

14. How nice you are to yourself in your head.

15. Whether you think positive or negative thoughts.

16. Whether or not you form expectations of people.

17. The type of food you eat.

18. When you answer someone's question (or email or call).

19. How much time you spend worrying.

20. How many new things you try.

21. How much exercise you get.

22. How many times you swear in traffic.

23. Whether or not you plan for the weather.

24. How much time you spend trying to convince people you're right.

25. How often you think about your past.

26. How many negative articles you read.

27. The attention you give to your loved ones when you see them.

28. How much you enjoy the things you have right now.

29. Whether or not you communicate something that's on your mind.

30. How clean or uncluttered you keep your physical space.

31. What books you read.

32. How well you network at social events.

33. How deeply you breathe when you experience stress.

34. How many times you admit you don't know something—and then learn something new.

35. How often you use your influence to help people instead of merely to build your influence.

36. When you ask for help.

37. Which commitments you keep and which you cancel.

38. How many risks you take.

39. How creative/innovative you are in your thinking.

40. How clear you are when you explain your thoughts.

41. Whether you formulate a new plan or act on your existing one.

42. How much information you get before you make a decision.

43. How much information you share with people.

44. Whether you smoke or drink (unless you're an alcoholic, in which case I am not qualified to offer you advice).

45. Whether or not you judge other people.

46. Whether you smell good or bad.

47. How much you believe of what other people say.

48. How quickly you try again after you fall.

49. How much rest you get at night.

50. How many times you say, "I love you."

ACKNOWLEDGMENTS

On *tinybuddha.com,* I've written that the website is not mine; it's ours—it's not about me; it's about us. The same is true for this book, and not just because readers and contributors submitted tweets for inclusion. This book would not exist if not for the loving, insightful community that makes Tiny Buddha what it is. First and foremost, I thank all of you for sharing yourselves so authentically and generously.

To my big fat Italian family, including but not limited to Kevin, Marianne, Tara, Ryan, Pauline, and Jeanne, thank you for loving me when I didn't love myself. Thank you especially, Mom and Dad, for letting me make a seemingly endless stream of massive mistakes when they couldn't have been easy to watch. They shaped my life and this book, and I'm grateful for every one of them.

To Ehren, thank you for being my best friend, my muse, and my eternal source of support, inspiration, and wisdom. I am a better person for knowing and loving you—and for following you out of that plane. A special thanks to my California family, including Pat, Cassie, Justin, and Jim for your endless generosity and kindness.

Thank you to Connie Chan for bringing yoga into my life and being a beacon of light for so many; to Jaime Case Ford for motivating me to pursue writing professionally; to Kevin Rose for teaching me to tweet and guiding me at many points along my journey; to Cori Poletto for designing the original *tinybuddha.com* and being a wonderful friend; to Joshua Denney for more than two years of design work, web strategy support, and general awesomeness; to Soren Gordhamer for encouraging the world to use technology a little more wisely and encouraging me to step out from the shadows; and thank you especially to Jan, Martha, Susie, Pat, and the team at Conari Press for believing in this project and bringing the world so many resources for happiness and positive change.

Wishing you health, happiness, peace, and love, my friends.

INDEX OF NAMES

ABOUT THE AUTHOR

Lori Deschene is the founder of *Tiny Buddha (tinybuddha.com)*, a community blog that features stories and insights from readers from all over the globe. She runs the site as a group effort because she believes we all have something to teach and something to learn. Since it launched in  2009, Tiny Buddha has grown into one of the most popular inspirational sites on the web, with over fifteen hundred contributors and more than two million monthly readers.

Lori is the author of *Tiny Buddha's Guide to Loving Yourself, Tiny Buddha's 365 Tiny Love Challenges,* and *Tiny Buddha's Gratitude Journal.* She's also co-founder of the online course *Recreate Your Life Story: Change the Script and Be the Hero.*

Formerly a writer for nationally distributed 'tween publications, she has also written articles for *Tricycle: The Buddhist Review, Shambhala Sun,* and *Chicken Soup for the Soul.*

A native of Massachusetts, Lori now lives in Los Angeles.

Photo by Ehren Prudhel

TO OUR READERS

Conari Press, an imprint of Red Wheel/Weiser, publishes books on topics ranging from spirituality, personal growth, and relationships to women's issues, parenting, and social issues. Our mission is to publish quality books that will make a difference in people's lives—how we feel about ourselves and how we relate to one another. We value integrity, compassion, and receptivity, both in the books we publish and in the way we do business.

Our readers are our most important resource, and we appreciate your input, suggestions, and ideas about what you would like to see published.

Visit our website, *www.redwheelweiser.com*, where you can subscribe to our newsletters and learn about our upcoming books, exclusive offers, and free downloads.

You can also contact us at *info@redwheelweiser.com*.

Conari Press
an imprint of Red Wheel/Weiser, LLC
65 Parker Street, Suite 3
Newburyport, MA 01950